D0707083

"Theologically rich. Profoundly God-centered. Unflinchingly honest. *Joy in the Sorrow* is a deeply moving account of how unexpected suffering undergirded by faith in Christ leads to joy and hope. I will carry these people, their stories, and their extraordinary joy with me for a long time; they have changed me. Buy this book, read it, and give it to those you love who are suffering."

VANEETHA RENDALL RISNER, Author,
The Scars That Have Shaped Me

"An incredible, personal, insightful journey led by one of my favorite teachers, Matt Chandler, as he and some of his friends share lessons brought to them by that greatest of all teachers in the Christian life—suffering. Martin Luther said that suffering, combined with prayer and meditation, is God's instrument to turn us into faithful theologians. You'll see that in this book, and you'll be changed yourself for the reading. Likely, you'll find yourself recommending it to someone even before you're finished."

J.D. GREEAR, President of the Southern Baptist Convention;
Pastor, The Summit Church, Durham, NC; Author, *Above All*

"Moving, inspiring, honest, and above all hope-filled. We must all walk through valleys in this life—and if you want to do so without losing joy and hope, then this is the book to read."

DR. TONY EVANS, Senior Pastor, Oak Cliff Bible Fellowship,
Dallas; President, The Urban Alternative

"An honest, searching, and in places deeply moving book, *Joy in the Sorrow* gives a dozen examples of how suffering can strike, and how God in Christ gets us through it. The stories are very different, but each one shows in its own way that whatever our circumstances, he is enough."

ANDREW WILSON, Teaching Pastor, King's Church London

"How does one face suffering with faith? Where do we quarry the resolve and courage? Is God good, even when the circumstances are not? Matt Chandler has wrestled with these questions. He addresses them with wisdom, love, and balance. This is a welcome book for all who suffer."

MAX LUCADO, Author, *Anxious for Nothing* and
Unshakable Hope

"This book helps us to see how we can look at whatever trials we may face in the light of Scripture and the gospel of Jesus Christ, and have confidence for ourselves or those we walk alongside in their sorrow, that God will use these things to grow our personal knowledge of him and will glorify Jesus through them. This book is best read before those sorrows come!"

BARBARA SHERWOOD, Navigators UK

"Prepare for your view of suffering to radically shift. *Joy in the Sorrow* will take you to some of your deepest places of sorrow—only to show you that even there, God is who he says he is, and God is right there with you in those times. I've watched Matt and Lauren live this, and those who know suffering make the best, most trusted teachers!"

JENNIE ALLEN, Founder and Visionary of IF:Gathering;
Author, *Nothing to Prove*

"In a day when empty words and false promises attempt to mask the realities of a suffering world, *Joy in the Sorrow* is a refreshingly honest look at the pain we face in our darkest hours and the unexpected hope and joy that can be found when Jesus meets us there. This book will breathe hope into your sufferings, deepen your understanding of God's purposes in them, and show you how true joy can be found not just after your sorrow but *within* it."

SARAH WALTON, Author, *Hope When It Hurts*

"I have long thought that the Western church doesn't have a theology of suffering—and we need one. Which is why I found this book so refreshingly honest, profound, thought-provoking, and ultimately beautifully hope-filled. The people in this book have all wrestled with doubts, cried countless tears, and mourned deeply—but have also found God to be profoundly real and close in their suffering. We can learn much from their experiences if we allow our hearts to be shaped as we read."

CLAIRE MUSTERS, Author, *Taking off the Mask*

MATT CHANDLER

AND FRIENDS

JOY

IN

THE

SORROW

The Village Church Resources™

thegoodbook COMPANY

Joy in the Sorrow: *How a Thriving Church
(and Its Pastor) Learned to Suffer Well*
© The Village Church, 2019

Published by:
The Good Book Company
in partnership with The Village Church

The Village
Church Resources™

thegoodbook.com | www.thegoodbook.co.uk
thegoodbook.com.au | thegoodbook.co.nz | thegoodbook.co.in

Unless otherwise indicated, Scripture quotations are from The Holy Bible, English
Standard Version (ESV), copyright © 2001 by Crossway, a publishing ministry of
Good News Publishers. Used by permission. All rights reserved.

All rights reserved. Except as may be permitted by the Copyright Act, no part of
this publication may be reproduced in any form or by any means without prior
permission from the publisher.

The Village Church has asserted its right under the Copyright, Designs and Patents
Act 1988 to be identified as author of this work.

ISBN (Hardcover): 9781784984229 (Paperback): 9781784983826 | Printed in India

Design by The Village Church / The Good Book Company

CONTENTS

When peace, like a river, attendeth my way,
When sorrows like sea billows roll;
Whatever my lot, Thou hast taught me to say,
It is well, it is well with my soul.

(Horatio G. Spafford, 1873)

PREFACE

Everyone will suffer. Yet there can be joy in our sorrow. No one in life—no matter who you are, no matter how big your bank account, no matter how great your health, no matter how much knowledge you have of God and the Bible, no matter how obedient you might be in your faith—can avoid suffering. If it hasn't come for you already, it will come soon enough. We've heard it said many times from the pulpit at The Village Church, but we're all just a phone call away from immense hurt and pain.

I say this to be realistic but not to be downbeat—because the very hope of this book is to tell you that even though we will all suffer, we can all find hope and purpose in that suffering. Through Jesus Christ and in the Scriptures, our suffering isn't just validated—it's addressed. God doesn't just say that we will suffer, but he teaches us something of why we suffer and much about how to suffer. And, even greater, he is the God who took the form of a human, a servant, and suffered on our behalf. God understands what it's like to be us. He gets our suffering. And he offers us joy in our sorrow.

I know that's my story, and it's why I felt compelled to help develop this book. Several years ago, within the span of twelve months, I experienced the hardest year of my life. I lost both my grandparents, my newborn daughter was fighting for her life, my dad suffered a massive heart attack that put him on life support and in a coma for nine days, and we got bed bugs in our house (that might sound minute compared to these other things, but do some googling). It was a dark, difficult, and disorienting time. My family was wounded and broken in more ways than one.

During that period, we often didn't know what to think or how to feel, yet there was a deep-seated joy and peace underneath those thoughts and feelings that sustained us and gave us life. God used years and years at The Village, including the story and sermons of Matt Chandler, and he used my closest family and community sitting with us, crying with us, praying for us, bringing us meals, and encouraging us in the Lord, to give us the faith that helped us walk through our suffering. Through it all, he gave us himself, his presence—he gave us joy.

So, in a sense, I feel as if I owe my life to the people of The Village. This book is just one tangible expression of my gratitude and my desire to take what I've seen and learned and share it with others. As I stepped into a new role at The Village to oversee the discipleship resources we create and share, this was the one project that I knew we had to do. I didn't have a choice. We didn't have a choice. This has been our story, and it's a story we've needed to share, in this way.

The pages that follow tell that story. You will hear from pastors and ministers and members, and former pastors and ministers and members, of The Village. Each chapter represents someone's story—and what God has shown that individual in and through their suffering—that has been a part of our bigger story here. Throughout the book, we also cut to excerpts from the video blogs—vlogs—that Matt recorded as he walked through his own suffering in the wake of collapsing with a brain tumor, and the subsequent surgery and treatment. Together, the stories are a reminder that we are people who have learned to suffer well together as we've walked together and leaned on the Lord together through so much.

As so many have said, suffering is the common denominator for all of humanity. Unfortunately, many churches and teachers today shy away from it altogether; and so when Christians enter into suffering, they have no framework for their pain and no foundation to stand on, and so they often run away from God amid the pain and sorrow, ending up in total despair. In drawing upon the Scriptures and our own experiences, it is our hope that we can help you, whether you're suffering right now, supporting someone who is, or simply looking to learn how to navigate whatever storm may come your way.

We obviously don't have it all figured out (no one will, this side of eternity), but we have found—albeit sometimes after much despair and heartache—that there can be real joy in our deepest pain. We hope and pray that you find that same joy when suffering comes your way, too.

David Roark, General Editor

1. I HAD NO ANSWERS

Joy in the Sorrow of Pastoring a Suffering Church

Matt Chandler

I don't think I'll ever forget the sights, sounds, and smells in that hospital room. The smell of latex, tiles, and cleaning supplies filled the air, while a mother, a father, and four grandparents grappled with the sorrow that comes when a baby is born with challenges that will keep him or her from living a "normal" life. There would be no baseball games or soccer tryouts. There would be no Friday night lights (that's Texas dialect for high school football). There would be no promise of a future.

It was the first time I ever saw an elderly man sob, and I felt completely discombobulated. The tiny baby boy had tubes and wires everywhere and laid in what looked to be a plexiglass coffin. I was in my first year at The Village Church in Dallas-Fort-Worth, a church of a few hundred members at that time. I was 28 years old with little pastoral experience and no seminary degree, and I was confused. How can God be glorified in a deadly birth defect in an infant? What is going on here? Between the sobs in the room and my head spinning with questions, I felt naked. I had no answers, and my heart was broken. I couldn't stop thinking about my own three-month-old daughter at home. What made everything worse was that I felt like I was supposed to be able to minister to my flock with some kind of confidence—and I couldn't.

A few weeks later, my phone rang around 8:30 a.m. I answered and heard a frantic voice on the line saying something I couldn't quite make out, except for the words "accident," "fishing," and "dead." A young couple from the church had gone to the Pacific Northwest to see some extended family and old friends and, most importantly, to introduce them to their newborn son. The husband and new daddy was a true outdoorsman. He had hiked multiple mountains in the United States and was an avid camper, hunter, and fisherman.

Early that morning in Oregon, he woke up and kissed his bride's forehead before quietly standing over his newborn son sleeping in the pack-and-play. Maybe he just stared at him, like new fathers tend to do. Having a son myself, I wonder if he was imagining the days when his boy would be getting up with him to hit the lake and see what good fortune might be waiting for them there. All we know about the accident is that the boat he and a couple of his friends were in capsized, and he drowned. A young man who hiked mountains, lived an active life, and was a great swimmer died that day. I still think about him. I even have a photo of him on the top of some mountain summit looking down on the valleys below. He loved Jesus, his wife, and his son. He was full of life, courage, and grit—a hard worker who would do anything for anyone in need. Why him? There are plenty of lazy, abusive, narcissistic men who neglect or hurt their families. Why not take them?

I could keep telling stories of the heartbreak and loss that seemed to mark my early years at The Village, but these two experiences highlight what is normative for everyone everywhere: the reality of a fallen world. I found myself longing to do the funeral of an 80-year-old grandparent who loved Jesus and faithfully served him until their dying breath, leaving a legacy of faith in their wake. But that wasn't my experience.

SUFFERING HEROES

Not long after that young husband's funeral, I decided that I was going to do a deep dive on suffering, so that I might better equip the men and women God had entrusted me to lead in how to think about suffering, and God's character and purposes in it—and, most of all, in how to face suffering when it came flooding into their lives. And notice that I say "when" and not "if" because all of us will suffer at some point; it's just a matter of when. I wanted to start with a biblical theology of suffering, leading me to dig into the Bible in search of how to make sense of the brokenness that seemed to be everywhere.

As I started to study, I realized that I had read a lot of my Bible without really paying attention to what I was reading.

Suffering in all forms was woven throughout the Scriptures—and not just in the book of Job. On almost every page there was disappointment, depression, doubt, sickness, and death. How had I missed it? I had been reading my Bible for over a decade and hadn't noticed that God's word had more to say about suffering in this life than I could ever have imagined. Sure, I knew Romans 8 v 28—"We know that for those who love God all things work together for good." I knew a smattering of other verses, including James 1 v 2-4:

> *Count it all joy, my brothers, when you meet trials of various kinds, for you know that the testing of your*

faith produces steadfastness. And let steadfastness
have its full effect, that you may be perfect and
complete, lacking in nothing.

But the raw pain, the heartbreak, and the disappointment in the stories of the Scriptures… I was seeing all that for the first time. It was as if I had been given new eyes.

In the Scriptures, there is suffering in almost every hero story. Joseph is sold into slavery, falsely accused, and forgotten in prison. Hagar is used as a commodity, has a child by Abraham, her master, and is then thrown out on her own. Moses roams the desert with grumbling complainers (church folk weren't much different back then) for 40 years only to not enter the promised land. Jeremiah is obedient to say the things the Lord commands him to and go to the places God sends him to, yet is beaten and left naked in a ditch. David spends years surrounded by enemies, not to mention suffering the gut-wrenching pain of his home life that dominated his later years. David, of course, is sinner as well as sinned against, as he summons Bathsheba to come to his palace and pressures her to commit adultery with him (in fact, if you look closely at what happened, it should be seen as rape). Paul is shipwrecked twice, beaten with rods and stones, suffers incessantly from what he calls his "thorn" (2 Corinthians 12 v 7), and is ridiculed incessantly. And at the center of our faith is a suffering Servant, a rejected Savior, a crucified King!

I could write a whole other chapter on the suffering of men and women who are barely mentioned in the Bible, or who aren't mentioned at all. Think for just a few moments about what normal life was like in Egypt under slavery, what life wandering in the desert was like, and the sheer volume of violence and death involved in entering the promised land. And what about the exiles? I assume some but not all of us can imagine what it was like to live on the margins under oppressive Babylon rule in the seventh century BC, and then under Roman rule in the first century.

The Bible isn't full of clean, happy living. You could argue that it's a book more full of tears than smiles. It's full of God working for the good of his people in the mess brought about by sin and death. God is with his people through suffering and through difficulty, so that they come out on the other side as a picture of grace and glory, and he uses them in their pain and changes the world through the results of their trials. You're not really thinking, "This person is going to be a big deal here"… and they become a big deal in God's story. Take Bathsheba again—taken advantage of by a powerful man, her king; and then God weaves her into the ancestry of the Son of God, her Savior and ours, the Lord Jesus. The suffering is not belittled, and the crime is not excused, yet God weaves it into his great story of salvation and hope.

We see the same thing throughout church history. Suffering is everywhere. Just to look back to the last 500 years and some of the more famous names, John Owen experienced the death of eleven children. Jonathan Edwards struggled with painful gout and then died at the young age of 55 after a smallpox inoculation had led to him contracting the disease shortly after he was named the president of Princeton University. Charles Spurgeon bore the weight of debilitating depression. John Calvin wrestled with digestion problems nearly his whole life. David Brainerd died of tuberculosis. And the list continues. To this day, most of the men and women I know whom God seems to be using in profound ways have endured or continue to endure "trials of various kinds." The 20th-century theologian A.W. Tozer once said, "It is doubtful whether God can bless a man greatly until he has hurt him deeply." At 43, I have seen this to be true.

But what I've found to be unique about the biblical perspective is not only that suffering is a reality but that joy in that suffering can be a reality too. James 1 not only assumes that we will face trials and tribulations as Christians but the author argues that these sufferings are a pathway to maturity, showing us that we lack nothing that we truly need. It's the idea that for us to bear fruit in our lives, we will probably need the plow. We need something to wake us up, to stir us up, to make us rely more on the Lord and look more like Jesus. And so when we walk into a trial, we can know "joy" there. There can be smiles in the tears.

Everyone will suffer. You're either suffering now, or you will be suffering in the future. As Christians, regardless of how faithful and obedient we are, we'll have seasons in which the sky is clear, and we'll have seasons in which it's cloudy. And one day we'll face the end of our seasons here. Everybody knows they're going to die, but nobody thinks it's this year. Nobody (unless they have a terminal diagnosis) thinks, "This is the year I'll die"—but I know that statistically somebody in my church, The Village, will die this year in their thirties or in their forties, out of nowhere. Nobody thinks that they're that somebody.

In dark and difficult seasons—when we face pain and suffering, when we get that one phone call that changes everything—we may not know or understand everything, but we can trust that the Lord is leading us into maturity and showing us that we need him. And we can also trust that, by his Spirit and through his church, he is not going to abandon us; he is with us. He is encouraging us and he is giving us what we need to walk through that suffering faithfully.

A THICK PEACE

When I began to read and study my Bible and make sense of these things, seeing the testimonies of those who suffered and what that suffering produced, I was eager to bring that into ministry at The Village. We were growing quickly. By my third year there, the Lord had blessed us with around 3,000 people. But I did not want us to grow in number anywhere near as much as I longed for us to grow in the maturity that James speaks of. I began teaching and training our young congregation that we would all suffer but that God could be trusted, that he was good and that he was at work in the mess. And as I taught these people, I learned from those people, as they walked through trials. I got to walk alongside them, as their pastor. And I got to see that Jesus makes a difference in those times.

One of the things I learned quickly, pastoring here in the early years, was that God gives you the grace when you need it, and not always before. Over and over and over again, I saw someone face their greatest fear—often their spouse or their child getting sick or dying suddenly—and over and over and over again, in that moment, I saw the grace of God show up, so that everything was still very difficult and very painful, but at the same time, the peace that surpasses all understanding was there. I've been trying to think of the right words to describe it, and I'm not sure I've managed, but it wasn't a light peace. There's a phrase from Paul's letter to the Philippian church that gets put up on Instagram all the time, and it is used often in times when nobody's suffering: "The peace of God, which surpasses all understanding, will guard your hearts and your minds in Christ Jesus" (Philippians 4 v 7). But this was that phrase being true when the suffering was deep—not a light peace, but a very thick peace. What I mean is that there was still a lot of sadness, a lot of heartbreak, a lot of disorientation—and yet there was also a confidence that God was working and that God was present in that suffering.

I saw the thick peace of God in hospital rooms, at funerals, in the daily trials of walking through valleys of struggle that seemed to have no end. I think that was one of the more significant revelations to me that I gained from watching believers suffer faithfully—that you're going to get the grace of God when you need it. I've heard other people say, "Oh man, I just don't think I could survive that," or, "Man, I don't know what I would do if that happened to me," and it's true—you don't know, unless it happens, and then the Lord provides for you. It's not five years later that God finally does his work. It's in that moment. He's there, but it's not a happy, skippity "He's here!" It's thicker than that. You're staggering, it's heartbreaking, but you know he's there; somehow you know he's good, and you know you're going to be alright.

I learned, from listening to and praying with and watching my brothers and sisters, that in the day of trouble, he'll be there. That doesn't mean the day of trouble's not a day of trouble. It really is a day of trouble. And that's where he meets us.

I think this is one of the things that is thin in evangelical thought today. We think God waits for us on the other side of hard things, and we're always looking for and celebrating the happy ending in this life. The stories we tell are usually finished stories. They have a bow on them. It's a rare thing for us to tell the story, right in the middle of doubt and anger and fear and confusion. Paul once wrote to his friends in Corinth that he was "afflicted in every way, but not crushed; perplexed, but not driven to despair" (2 Corinthians 4 v 8). We don't like to spend a lot of time with those words "afflicted" and "perplexed." We like to hurry up and get to the "not crushed." "I don't get it, God." "Why is this happening, God?" Nobody likes to camp out there for a while. But Paul felt like that—he had seen Jesus face to face, he had been to the third heaven, he'd told dead people to stop being dead, and yet there were parts of what God was doing that were perplexing to

Paul. They didn't crush him or drive him to despair—but they were confusing. If Paul can be confused, then certainly there's space for us to be confused. But, as with Paul, joy and sorrow can co-exist for the Christian. We can be totally confused, and yet at peace, at the same time. It's a paradox, but I watched it in real life again and again.

THE SUFFERING MEGACHURCH

And so this teaching, and a robust theology of suffering, became foundational to the life of our church, in what we were saying and how we were living. It was at the same time as we were growing seriously fast that many of us were seriously suffering. And I think that is right and good.

My heart is always to let the Bible define reality for us, rather than having to take reality and manipulate it to make it something that it's just not. It doesn't make any sense to try to hide suffering and brokenness, when it's clearly a part of life in this world; and when it's clearly a part of the gospel that Jesus is with us in the mess, in the storms, and in the pain. Any message that says, "These things aren't real" or "You need to have more faith to not have these things" might be a popular one, but it is also a disingenuous one that ultimately stands opposed to truth. If you're not real about the reality of sorrow, you end up creating guilt and shame in people around suffering.

One of the things that I think drew people to The Village is a phrase that we said years ago that took on a life of its own: "It's okay to not be okay; it's just not okay to stay there." We wanted to be honest not just about suffering, but even about failure. We wanted to cultivate an environment where we could be human on earth, in a broken and fallen world. We didn't want to teach or operate in a way that denies the reality of sin and suffering, that suggests that somehow our pain and failures take away from the glory of

God. We wanted to proclaim the belief that God's glory actually works itself out in the trials and sufferings of humankind. It's why when our leadership has made mistakes, we step up on stage and say, "We've sinned against you. Please forgive us." Everything—from suffering to ways that we as a leadership have sinned—we've tried to own, not run away from. We've tried to create a culture that acknowledges that brokenness is a part of our existence, but that also remembers that God's at work in that mess. In a church like that, people begin to feel safe, and they begin to enter into community—they begin to enter into deeper relationships. They're freed from the idea that "No suffering, no difficulty, no struggle" is mature Christianity. That view traps you into a fakeness and a performance, and stops you being real, finding grace from God, getting help from others, and walking forward with real joy.

So we became a people who knew well where suffering fits into the Scriptures and into our lives. We grew in number, but we grew in depth, too. Even as we reached 7,000 members, we continued to be very real about our flaws and our difficulties. Other people described us as a successful church, but not many realized that we were also a joyfully suffering church—and that, really, those two things are the same. And one of the greatest ironies and joys of my life is that while I was preparing to help our people suffer, God was preparing me to suffer.

There I was, teaching everybody to be prepared to suffer well, and I had no idea that I was being prepared. I didn't know that the Lord was saying, *Matt, you're going to need to study a little more. Hey, pay attention to this; you're going to need this.* I was thinking, *The people here need this.* The Lord knew, *Yeah, but you're not separate from them, Matt. You need this.*

"People described
us as a successful
church, but not many
realized we were also
a joyfully suffering
church—and that,
really, those two
things are the same."

#JOYINTHESORROW

THANKSGIVING DAY 2009

On Thanksgiving Day 2009, I woke up to the smell of coffee and cinnamon rolls. My wife, Lauren, had graciously let me sleep in and had already run to the store to pick up those small items that you tend to forget. The house was full of the joyful noises that accompany a day of feasting and playing. The kids were laughing at something in the living room, and I could hear the squeak, squeak, squeak of the springs on my youngest's "Johnny Jump Up." I hugged Lauren as I walked into the kitchen and poured myself a cup of coffee. She asked if I could give Norah her bottle while she finished putting together some dishes for lunch later that day.

I walked into the living room and put my coffee down and fed Norah her bottle. She was six months old at the time and would stare at me with an occasional smile as she drank.

I burped her.

I took her back to her Johnny Jump Up.

I turned to head back to my chair.

And that's my last memory before waking up in the hospital.

SUDDENLY IT'S YOU

And so suddenly it was me looking over the precipice of this life. I wasn't walking alongside those in our church who were suffering anymore. I was the one walking through the valley. I was the one in the hospital, wondering how much brain function I'd have on the other side. I was the one hearing, "You've probably got two or three years, and those years are going to be pretty awful." It's a super lonely place—your wife can be there with you, your kids can be around you, your best friends can support you. But it's not them—it's you.

This book is about what happened to me and in me after that Thanksgiving Day—how the Lord showed up, and what he did, and what I learned. But more, much

26

more than that, it's about those who I have learned from. It's the stories of the precious brothers and sisters who taught me in their lives how to suffer well. Some of them taught me before I stood on the precipice; others continue to display God's grace in their sorrow. It's the accounts of how the Lord showed up in their lives. It's the story of how, through their faithfulness and joy in the valley, they showed their church—and taught (and continue to teach) their pastor—how to suffer well.

From Matt's Vlog
December 7, 2009
(Eleven days after Thanksgiving)

Hi, I'm Matt Chandler. If you haven't heard, it's been quite the week for us.

On Thanksgiving morning I had a seizure and woke up in the hospital. They did some scans, and they found a tumor on my right frontal lobe. It's about two inches in diameter by one inch deep. On Friday they're going to go in and cut it out—and so I wanted to say just a couple of things to you very quickly.

One, I just can't thank you enough—the places where our hearts have been real tender is the outpouring of love and encouragement and support and prayers, not just from The Village Church but all over the world; and that's been such a humbling, humbling thing to me and my family. And so I wanted to thank you for that.

And then the second thing I wanted to say is that when I've been on my travels this fall, I have been preaching out of Hebrews 11. And in Hebrews 11 the writer says that some of God's people shut the mouths of lions and some put foreign armies to flight, and it goes through all these good things that happened to these people of God—and then right in the middle, in verse 36, it just turns and it says "[and] others suffered mocking and flogging … they were stoned, they were sawn in two, they were … destitute." And then he says *both* walked in faith.

Now I'm 35 years old, and at this point in my life all God's ever given me is… well, we've "stopped the mouths of lions" and we've "put foreign armies to flight," and we've fought against injustice, and there has been nothing but good that has come to me. And so I've always felt like, when I taught that message, there was this hitch in me: because when I said, "But some don't get those things, and that's OK," I thought there would be people in the crowd who would say, "Well, of course you're going to say that. Of course you're going to, because God's done nothing but be good to you. He's done nothing but be gracious. He's done nothing but let you have victory after victory after victory." And so when this all came out—when we were expecting to get multiple options from the surgeon and we got, "There's one option—we need you to get in there *now*"—there's this part of me that's so grateful that the Lord counted me worthy for this, and there's this part of me that goes, "OK," because now in an area where it's not a big win, I get to show that he's enough. I get to praise him and exalt him and make much of him in *this*. He's counted me worthy to point to him in *this*.

Now know that we've cried our tears at my house, and I've held my children, and I've kissed them, and I've kissed my wife. Know that what I would love is to be a 70-year-old man drinking a coffee. I would love to walk my daughter down the aisle. I would love to see my boy turn into the athlete I never was. I would love to do all of that—but none of those things is better than him. None of those things is—and I'm saying that *now*, I'm saying that *right now*: not as the guy who has everything and has nothing in front of him that he could lose—

I'm telling you that, now that I'm a guy who could lose everything in an instant.

I love you; I love The Village. It's been the great joy of my life to yell at you for seven years, and my plan is to come back—and we'll see what the Lord has for me.

I am not afraid. And so for those of you who just keep living in fear, and you would try to use this as an excuse to continue in that fear—don't you dare use me as an excuse to continue in that. My hope would be that you would see that God is good in all things, and that he would never send to any of us things he does not provide strength for. I love you more than you know, and I can't wait to be back. I love you.

2. BEAUTY IN THE RIPPLES

Joy in the Sorrow of a Teenage Son's Accident

Jeanne Damoff

When you're reading a suspenseful story, are you tempted to flip ahead and find out what's going to happen? With books, we have the luxury of being able to read the ending first, or skip the parts that make us uncomfortable, or (if we really don't like the way things are shaping up) we can toss the book aside and choose one that is more suited to our preferences.

At times I've wished my life could be like that.

AN AUTHOR WITH PURPOSE

Every story has a beginning, a middle, and an end, and every person has a story. In one sense, that story began at birth, but really, it began long before that, in the heart of the Author.

Psalm 139 v 16 says of God that "in your book were written, every one of them, the days that were formed for me, when as yet there was none of them." God writes our stories before we're born. The whole thing: beginning, middle, and end. From our perspective, life unfolds with day-to-day choices and challenges, but nothing that happens takes him by surprise. And the Author of our life stories writes with purpose.

But sometimes life doesn't feel like a loving Author penned its pages. We live in a broken world. Our lives are touched by suffering, disease, betrayal, bereavement, loneliness, and grief. When we find ourselves in the midst of deep pain, our natural reaction is to ask "Why?" If God is in control, why doesn't he fix this mess? Why do good people get sick and die? Why are innocent children abandoned or abused? How could all this apparent chaos be part of his plan?

I can't offer tidy answers, but I can offer something even better: hope. We live in a broken world, but we live here by the purposeful design of a redeeming God. When he writes pain into our stories, he also reveals himself as the main character. Sure, he's been there all along in our joys and delights, but suffering is unique in its power to tune our souls to his presence.

I once spent an afternoon on the Stanford University campus in Palo Alto, California, and a highlight of my day was touring the Memorial Church there. I tiptoed down the aisles, snapping photographs and admiring the architecture and the craftsmanship of the mosaics and stained-glass windows. Reminiscent of a European cathedral, it was all very exquisite, ornate, and awe-inspiring. But one thing I saw stopped me in my tracks.

A large block of stone served as a foundation for the pulpit, and these words were etched on it:

It is by suffering that God has most nearly approached to man; it is by suffering that man draws most nearly to God.

When I read those words, I thought about how God drew nearest to man through the suffering and death of his Son, and how suffering in my own life—especially in what has happened to my son—has revealed God in ways nothing else ever could.

LEARNING IN THE FIRE

Several biblical metaphors help me understand the purposeful ways in which God deals with his children through pain and suffering. The prophets Isaiah (48 v 10), Zechariah (13 v 9), and Malachi (3 v 3) all depicted God as a refiner, purifying his beloved ones through the fire of affliction. Isaiah (29 v 16), Jeremiah (18 v 6), and Paul (Romans 9 v 20-21) compared God to a masterful potter, and his people to clay—his to shape and mold as he wills. Jesus portrayed his Father as a wise gardener, who prunes us that we might bear more fruit (John 15 v 1-2).

The things we learn in the divine Refiner's fire can't be learned anywhere else. We need the pressure of the Potter's hand. We need the severe mercy of the pruning shears. Whatever God has ordained for us today is for our good: not only the things that are fun and comfortable, but the fire as well. For only when the gold has been purified can it reflect the Refiner's face.

The natural reaction to pain and suffering may be to ask "Why?", but when someone who loves us gives us a gift we don't question their motive. We say "Thank you." It's not that we enjoy suffering, but that we trust the unchanging love of the Potter, the Gardener, our merciful Refiner. If we accept suffering as a gift and express gratitude for it—offering a sacrifice of praise—then hope is born.

Real hope is not a guarantee of certain outcomes in this life, but rather the assurance that the One who is perfectly wise and perfectly good holds the outcomes in his almighty hand. The Heidelberg Catechism, a Protestant confessional document written in 1563, is a series of questions and answers used for teaching biblical truths. It begins with this question: "Christian, what is your only comfort in life and death?"

The response goes like this:

That I am not my own, but belong body and soul, in life and in death, to my faithful Savior Jesus Christ.

He has fully paid for all my sins with his precious blood, and has set me free from the tyranny of the devil. He also watches over me in such a way that not a hair can fall from my head without the will of my Father in heaven; in fact, all things must work together for my salvation.

Because I belong to him, Christ, by his Holy Spirit, assures me of eternal life and makes me wholeheartedly willing and ready from now on to live for him.

That is comforting, isn't it? God is near. He numbers the hairs on our heads. "Are not two sparrows sold for a penny? And not one of them will fall to the ground apart from your Father" (Matthew 10 v 29).

His eye is on the sparrow. We love that image. But I think we can easily miss an important aspect of this promise. The verse doesn't say that sparrows won't fall, but that God is there—aware and in control—when they do.

So, what are we to do when our Father allows our own precious sparrow to drop from the sky?

Everyone has a story. You have one, and so do I. Some of the chapters in my story read like a fairytale frolic in flowery meadows, and some are like walking barefoot over shards of glass. If it had been up to me, I would have left those painful chapters out, but as I look back over my life, I realize they truly are gifts from a good God who never calls us to suffer without purpose.

THE DAY "HAPPILY EVER AFTER" VANISHED

If you drop a pebble in water, ripples are set in motion. But let's say it's not a pebble. Let's say it's a priceless jewel. Something you dearly love. Something irreplaceable. You've spent your life trying to protect it, and now, due to circumstances beyond your control, it's gone. You stare in disbelief at the spot where it went down, a multitude of "if only's" swirling in your head. You wish you could press rewind or wake up and realize it's all just a horrible nightmare. But you can't, because it isn't.

At this point, you have a choice. You can keep staring at the spot where your treasure sank, or you can watch the ripples to see what God is doing. Because God is always doing something beautiful. And he wants you to see it.

When our son Jacob was 15, he went missing at an end-of-school lake party. When he was found on the bottom of the lake, he had been under water for at least 10 minutes, and it took another 20 minutes of CPR before he breathed. Doctors told us he would either die or remain vegetative for the rest of his life.

Life as we'd known it ended that day. Happily ever after vanished in the mist, replaced by crushing agony and a million questions. If God loves us and is in control, how could he let this happen? How could this be his plan for our son? Our family? Our future?

Almost immediately, we saw God at work in and through our suffering. We saw him meeting our needs and touching the lives of those who came alongside us, and the more time passed, the more beauty he revealed. But still. My treasure was gone. My beautiful, brilliant son was in a coma. And my heart was shattered.

I imagine there will be those who read these words whose hearts are as raw right now as mine was then—with pain so deep that it hurts to breathe. You wonder if you'll ever

"In the past, you understood intellectually that every breath was grace. Now you're living it."

J O Y I N T H E S O R R O W

feel happiness again—if you'll ever really laugh with your whole body and soul. I wondered those things. And I wondered how belief in God's goodness and all this agony could co-exist in my one small heart. And yet, at the same time, I sensed his strong arm holding me securely and sustaining me moment by moment.

It's a bit of a paradox when you find yourself clinging to the very God who is putting you through the fire. In these times, all of life is distilled to its essence. Priorities shift. Things that once seemed extremely important fade into the background, and eternal matters take center stage. In the past, you understood intellectually that every breath was grace. Now you're living it.

If that's you, and even if it isn't, I want to encourage you today. If you've been called by God and are a follower of Christ, he is working "all things … together for good" in your life (Romans 8 v 28). Real good—by his definition of the word, not yours or mine. If we filter the word "good" through a worldly lens, then we might assume we're promised material success or respect in our work, or that God has to give us that one thing we've been asking for, because obviously it's a good thing. But if we use a biblical lens, we realize that the good he promises may be the suffering or trial or persecution that he knows we need to be conformed to the image of his Son, and that is our greatest possible good.

As a Christian, the word of God tells me that every difficulty, sorrow, or loss that touches my life will ultimately be redeemed and transformed into a gift, but I have to choose to see it that way. I choose my response: resentment or trust? A stubborn "Why?" that refuses any answer but the one it wants? Or a deliberate "Thank you" that believes and confesses that God is good even if a thousand questions remain?

Am I saying that God is the author of evil? No, but I am saying that he is enthroned above it—and that, ultimately, even evil must serve his purpose.

SOMETHING BETTER THAN ANSWERS

Scripture is full of stories that illustrate this reality, and Job is a perfect example. Satan demanded to test Job, confident that suffering would turn him away from God. God gave Satan permission to afflict Job, but the events that followed were not the result of a casual celestial wager. Remember, it was God who initiated the conversation in the first place, bringing Job to Satan's attention. God exploited Satan's pride, using him as a tool for furthering God's will in Job's life. A loving Father was refining his child, for his good.

Compared to others, Job was a prime specimen of godliness and goodness, and his initial response to his suffering was a stunning declaration of faith:

> *"Naked I came from my mother's womb, and naked shall I return. The LORD gave, and the LORD has taken away; blessed be the name of the LORD." In all this Job did not sin or charge God with wrong.*
> *(Job 1 v 21-22)*

But this posture of unquestioning acceptance didn't last. The intense fires of suffering made spiritual pride rise to the surface, where God could skim it off. And when God finally did respond to Job's self-justifying questions, he offered no answers. None. He simply revealed himself, and that was enough. Once Job saw God for who he is, all his demands for answers fell silent. And in the end, his humility and faith brought more glory to God than he ever would have been able to bring as a self-righteous man inundated with blessings. Job's refined character reflected holy reverence and dependence. He became a man fit to stand in God's presence (Job 42 v 7-9).

It's interesting to note that throughout his ordeal, Job never saw behind the veil into the spiritual battle in the heavens. He saw only the devastating circumstances of his life. He never got answers to his questions. But he got something much better: a revelation of God himself. God was purposeful in Job's suffering, and he is purposeful in ours, too—even when our questions go unanswered.

Peace comes from trusting God, even when I can't understand his ways. When I cry out to him in my sorrow, he draws near, lifting me above my earthly desires and expectations, and tuning my heart to the eternal. When I encounter suffering I didn't think I could handle—when I have to confront the thing I dreaded most—it presses me into prayer. And through it all, I'm conformed to the image of Christ.

WHAT IS YOUR PRAYER FOR YOUR CHILDREN?
Sometimes we can only trust that the ripples are there—seen by God but hidden to us. But sometimes the veil brushes aside, and we catch glimpses of the redemption God intended all along.

It's been 23 years since Jacob's near-drowning. Despite doctors' predictions, over the course of a year he did awaken from his coma—a miracle by all accounts. He can walk and talk, and joyful faith is the hallmark of his life. But his brain injury limits him to a very simple, dependent life. He'll probably never marry. Never have his own home or a real job. Never experience most of the things the world associates with success.

I struggled with this for a long time. Yes, I'd seen glimpses of good and beauty in the ripples, I'd felt real gratitude, and I'd come to a place of peace—but I still grieved for what Jacob and our family had lost.

One day, when sadness had swamped me yet again, I asked God to help me understand how this could be his will for Jacob. Then I felt as if he asked me a question: *What is your prayer for your children?*

I said, "When they stand in your presence, I want them to hear you say, 'Well done, good and faithful servant.'"

And it was as though God said, *Look at him. He loves me with all his heart, and everyone who sees him is drawn to me. He is my faithful servant.*

What does it matter that Jacob will never impress the world with his accomplishments? He delights the One who created him for his own pleasure and glory, and his life is a shining portrait of redemption. What more could I ask for my son?

When we suffer, we have a choice: turn our focus inward and be consumed with self-pity and bitterness or lift our eyes and watch the Redeemer make all things new. Yes, we grieve. We wouldn't be human if we felt nothing. Even Jesus wept (John 11 v 35). But we can still choose to believe in God's goodness and give thanks in the midst of our grief. And when we look for his hand in the ripples, we begin to see him everywhere.

When Jacob was in a coma, many prayed for him and our family. We felt the power of those prayers, and it was humbling and overwhelming. I remember how helpless I felt, wishing there were some way I could repay all those people or at least thank them, but I had no way of even knowing who they were. So I did the only thing I could think of. I returned the favor.

I asked God to draw near to anyone who prayed for Jacob, and I prayed he would meet them in ways in which they'd never experienced him before. I asked him to answer their prayers for us but also to meet their own deepest needs. Praying that way brought me much joy, and eventually

I began to hear stories that gave me reason to believe God was answering.

HIS ARMS WILL CATCH IT ALL

At the time of Jacob's near-drowning, my husband, George, was a biology professor at East Texas Baptist University. Several months later, when the fall semester started, he spoke in a chapel service to let the college community know ways they could minister to Jacob and our family. He requested prayer and also that anyone who felt so inclined would visit Jacob in the nursing facility where he was receiving care. He was still officially in a coma, and stimulation was good for him. George invited people to read aloud, sing, pray, rub his hands and feet—whatever they felt comfortable doing.

Many responded, and soon an army of volunteers marched in and out of that little room. They poured love on a boy who couldn't give anything in return, and left with the kind of joy only an encounter with the living God can give—a stunning display of beauty and purpose.

One of the students present in the chapel service was a young mom with children of her own. She knew she wouldn't have time to visit Jacob, but she committed to pray for him every day. Late one evening, she returned home to a messy house. In her weariness and frustration, she considered skipping prayer. But a sense of urgency prompted her to shut out the mess and pray for Jacob.

No sooner had she bowed her head than the words and music to a song filled her mind. She snatched paper and pencil and wrote as fast as she could. When the pencil finally fell silent, she wrote a title at the top—"Jacob's Song":

> *Sometimes there's just no way to explain it all*
> *And we question, "Lord, why is this the path that I*
> *must walk?"*

Though the shadows fall across our way
We must know that there's a better day

He's the healer; He's the keeper
He's the One who makes it all
And when you get to the end of your rope,
Just let go and fall
For his arms will catch it all

Remember a special time of peace from days ago
Now imagine a greater peace than you have ever known
This peace awaits your soul
You only must let go

Still yet, we hope and pray, and we watch for signs
But we know in our own hearts is where the healing
lies
There is more God wants to say
That is why he remolds the clay

He's the healer; He's the keeper
He's the One who makes it all
And when you get to the end of your rope,
Just let go and fall
For his arms will catch it all
For his arms will catch us all

The next day, she dropped by George's office with her guitar
and played it for him. He asked her to go to our home and
play it for me. That November, she and I sang it together
in a citywide Thanksgiving service for an auditorium full of
people who'd been praying for and ministering to our family
over the past six months. The Lord's presence was palpable.

And the ripples continued.

SEEING THE RIPPLES

A couple of years later, that same student was asked to sing at a Christmas party for patients, their families, and staff at the Baylor Institute of Rehabilitation in Dallas, Texas. She had no idea that Jacob had spent two months in BIR's coma treatment program the summer after the accident.

After singing some Christmas carols, she decided to perform "Jacob's Song." As she told the story behind the song, a couple of staff members whispered to one another, "Do you think she means our Jacob?"

When the song was over, they slipped out to find Dr. Mary Carlile. A nationally respected brain-injury expert, Dr. Carlile had been Jacob's primary physician at BIR, and he'd had a profound impact on her life. Given the circumstances of his accident, she'd been unable to offer us any hope of recovery. Believing he would either die or remain vegetative, she said the kindest thing we could do would be to remove his feeding tube and let him die.

This advice was not given coldly. Dr. Carlile had wept beside Jacob's bed. She and her team had done everything possible to protect his body from the deforming contracture common in those who suffer severe brain injury. But facts were facts. A brain can't survive for more than 10 minutes without oxygen.

Except that Jacob's had.

When Jacob walked back into BIR a year later, the whole place erupted into celebration. And from that day onward when counseling families, Dr. Carlile never again used the words "no hope." Medical science, she'd tell them, doesn't have the last word: God does.

That day in December, she followed the staff members back to the party room, and they requested the song again. BIR adopted it for use in their music-therapy program, and Dr. Carlile took a CD home. As her own mother suffered through the illness that eventually took her life, Jacob's Song became one of her greatest comforts.

These were some of the ripples we did get to see. Beautiful, purposeful, redemptive ripples expanding outward and reaching far beyond the scope of our view—our suffering not only being transformed into a gift to us, but to many.

And there were more. Seven years after Jacob's accident, I knew it was time to write a book about our family's journey and all the ways that God had redeemed our brokenness—to encourage others who, like me, longed to find meaning in their pain. But I wanted to capture the broader scope of his purposes, so I wrote letters to people who'd been a part of our story, asking them to share how God had used these events in their lives.

I sent those letters to family members, Jacob's friends, his long-time aide, doctors, church leaders, college students, and community members who had witnessed and participated in Jacob's gradual awakening. And then I waited.

As their replies began to trickle back in, I wept in amazement and awe. Those stories showed me that God had done and was continuing to do far more than I'd ever imagined. They gave me glimpses into the bigger picture of his eternal purposes that I never would have known about if I hadn't asked. The ripples had continued to spread. And they are still spreading.

Since the book, *Parting the Waters*, was released, my prayer has been much the same as it was before—that God would meet people as they enter the pages of our story in ways they've never experienced him before. That he would hear the deepest cries of their hearts, and they'd begin to see him in the ripples of their own lives. Just as I received letters before, now I receive testimonies from readers, and my heart overflows with gratitude. In his wisdom, our redeeming, refining God marked out a path I never would have chosen, and I know the ripples from Jacob's life will keep spreading outward and accomplishing God's purposes until they finally reach the other shore.

MOVING BEYOND THE WHY

This is not just true for our story. It's true for you, too, and for everyone who places their hope in God through Christ.

You may be reading these words and longing to see God in the ripples of your life. Maybe you're longing for that hope but don't know how to find it. Life has been so crowded with "Why?" that there hasn't been any room for "Thank you."

Romans 5 v 1-10 says:

> *Therefore, since we have been justified by faith, we have peace with God through our Lord Jesus Christ. Through him we have also obtained access by faith into this grace in which we stand, and we rejoice in hope of the glory of God. Not only that, but we rejoice in our sufferings, knowing that suffering produces endurance, and endurance produces character, and character produces hope, and hope does not put us to shame, because God's love has been poured into our hearts through the Holy Spirit who has been given to us.*
>
> *For while we were still weak, at the right time Christ died for the ungodly. For one will scarcely die for a righteous person—though perhaps for a good person one would dare even to die—but God shows his love for us in that while we were still sinners, Christ died for us. Since, therefore, we have now been justified by his blood, much more shall we be saved by him from the wrath of God. For if while we were enemies we*

"Even though you
don't know how the
rest of your life will
unfold, you can read
the ending. If Jesus
is your Lord, 'Happily
ever after' will be
yours in the end."

#JOYINTHESORROW

*were reconciled to God by the death of his Son, much
more, now that we are reconciled, shall we be saved
by his life.*

Remember that stone foundation? "It is by suffering that God
has most nearly approached to man." For while we were weak,
Christ died for us. "It is by suffering that man draws most
nearly to God." We can rejoice even in our sufferings.

You really can move beyond the "Why" that has kept
your eyes glued to the spot where your treasure sank beneath
the waves, and turn your gaze to the "Thank you" that is
riding the ripples. Even though you don't know how the rest
of your life will unfold, you actually can flip ahead and read
the ending. If Jesus is your Lord, then he has promised to
come back for you, and when he does, he will wipe every
tear from your eyes (Revelation 21 v 4). "Happily ever after"
will be yours in the end.

Christ suffered and died to draw near to you. He rose
from the dead to deliver you from death's power. He sees
your heart. He knows your pain. And he longs to redeem it.
If you don't yet know him, you can come exactly as you are
to receive his mercy and his hope. Indeed, you can't come
any other way. He already knows your story. He wrote it.

And today can be the start of a brand new chapter.

December 23, 2009

The tumor that they took out of my brain—and it's hard to believe it's two weeks ago now—ended up being anaplastic, or malignant. And so it's been an interesting three weeks for my family and me, in regards to our spirit, in regards to just talking and wrestling and looking at life and looking at eternity. And looking at all of that, the verse that's been constantly in my head is out of Ecclesiastes, where it says:

> *"It is better to go to the house of mourning*
> *than to go to the house of feasting,*
> *for this is the end of all mankind,*
> *and the living will lay it to heart." (7 v 2)*

I think the reason that's really been on our hearts and in my own mind is because I've made no secret over the last few years of preaching that I think most men are wooed and seduced into lives that don't matter, concentrating on things that are temporary and frivolous, and so one of the reasons why something like this in my own life and in the church's life is going to be good for all of us is that we get the veil of mortality lifted a little bit, so we can see clearly, "Oh, there is an end to all men."

So I love you, I'm looking forward to getting back—we're already starting to talk about what it looks like for me to come back. I'm ready to preach, so we're working through those details now.

Just to tell you what's coming up in the future, and we'll divulge more of this as it gets set, it looks like I've got chemotherapy and radiation coming my way from the first of the year for a decent, extended period of time. We'll do that, and we'll see how everything responds. My plan is to be your pastor for a long, long, long time. I can't thank you enough for all the encouragement and prayers—the peace and the joy we are walking in in all of this is, I think, just absolutely woven into how many of you guys are praying for us and asking the Lord to give us that peace—asking the Lord to give us that confidence in him—so thank you for that. I'm looking forward to reading the letters and reading the cards, and we've started a little system at the house to go through those. So, I love you guys very much—please continue to pray for us, and we'll continue to let you know what's going on.

3. TREASURE VEILED
IN HEARTACHE

Joy in the Sorrow of a Wife's Death

Guy Delcambre

It was a day like any other: ordinary, just as I had come to expect. For me life was easy, predictable, and measured. Whatever difficulty I did encounter, I could handle. I was in control.

And then, right there in the middle of an ordinary day, all that was suddenly turned over. The life that I once knew and loved deeply no longer existed. And that is the sting of suffering: in the disorientation left in its wake, nothing feels certain.

My phone buzzed as it received a text message from my sister. "Is everything okay with Marianne?" I had not been home or spoken with my wife since leaving for work earlier that morning. Figuring that a misunderstanding between them must have occurred, and given that I was only ten minutes from home, I decided the text message could go unanswered for the moment. And then an incoming call from my wife's phone. A delayed start and then the shaky voice of my wife's mother.

"She had a seizure and… the ambulance is taking her."

Not many more words were exchanged. The tension hanging between those words said enough. Without hesitation, I re-routed to the hospital.

Marianne and I met at a time when so much in our lives was just beginning to settle. Both of us were drawn to living lives full of meaning and purpose. Life was an adventure to be had, full of memories waiting to be made. And the more we learned about one another, and learned that we had a very deep mutual affection, the more we knew that we would go into the adventure together. Our conversations often dreamed about what it meant to truly care for people, and this led us to pastoral ministry. We lived many of those dreams and more. As the years together piled on, many adventures were shared, one of them being starting a family. We had three healthy daughters, each one different and unique. Life was good and normal and fairly easy to manage. This was the dream that I thought of as the good life.

All of these thoughts flashed through my mind as I sped to the hospital, never thinking for a moment that an end was what I would arrive to find.

"Sir, are you okay? Do you understand what I'm saying? Do you have this information?" The voice of a nurse began to break into my awareness. Her rapid-fire questioning gave me cause for worry: that, and the tubes running out of my wife's body. As medical staff rushed around the room, I stood still, immobilized by the thought that things were certainly not all right. In what felt like an instant, suffering poured into my life like a storm surge, pushing into places where floodwaters should not be.

Days crept by—days of little, insignificant gains. People were praying, and doctors were pulling out all the stops, researching possible solutions to help my wife turn a corner that we would soon learn she never would. Those days were insufferably long and difficult. The pity housed in the eyes of those we loved was hard to look at.

It is a peculiarly intimate horror to slowly lose half of yourself. After five dwindling days in the ICU, my wife exhaled all of this life that was left within her body and entered another realm.

I wasn't ready.

A LIFE FAMILIAR, BUT ALTOGETHER DIFFERENT

In the weeks and months that followed, I became a citizen of two worlds: one was the life I knew and loved; the other was stretched out before me as a land that was both eerily familiar and also altogether different. After Marianne's death, little made sense or held a purpose that I could perceive. Everything that once gave me cause for joy and value dissipated along with the undisturbed life that I once knew. It was as though suffering displaced me, usurped all happiness, and drained reason from my heart. What drew me back were the three little faces that still held her glow. Our little daughters, whose hearts wilted in grief, would serve as the way that God would restart my heart.

I remember all too well our first conversation after their mother's death. We hadn't seen each other for five days. In fact, the last time we had seen each other was a lifetime ago, when we were still all together, all five of us. Now we were four. And I was the only one of us aware of that.

My sister had been caring for our daughters while their mother left this life. As I approached my sister's house, I knew that I could not in any way change what had happened. I could not stop, slow, or divert death's taking. No words came to mind to adequately explain to them what had happened.

They knew I was soon to arrive, and in preparation for the occasion, had thoughtfully created Get Well signs, adorned with lovingly scribbled drawings and messages for their mother. Of course, they expected her to be home soon, the five of us all to be reunited and secure—just how things should be and as life had always been. But there would be no comforting words in our reunion—only the announcement of a new, unchosen life where death had pulled away what we would never have given.

As they heard me voice the words that she had died, I watched the light in their little eyes dim and listened to their little hearts shake under the weight of suffering.

And to this day, years into a new life, I can still see their lives quake at times.

Grief is not some sort of precisely specified process map, beginning at point A and moving measuredly on to point B for completion. Rather, grief is a lifelong journey that is traveled patiently, steadily, and little by little. This is what we have come to learn: God is faithful, immeasurably so, and in ways we can never fully fathom. And just as God is faithful, he is merciful in his determination to bring about the plans that he has for our lives. The path does not always make sense or fit within our planned-out futures. We are only invited to follow it and, as pilgrims, sojourn through this land.

I WANTED MY LIFE BACK

When I think back, I see two men both striving for the same thing: security. My wife had suddenly died, my daughters were haunted by her instant and absolute removal from their little lives, and I was lost, wondering how life could go so wrong so quickly and why God had allowed this to be. The two men were a man of faith and a man clinging to a life now gone. They both worked hard to plot a course. Emotions swirled furiously. One moment I prayed, and in the next pulled breath I cursed the reason for prayer. I wanted my neatly-folded life back. Instead, each day fell clumsily into the next. Despite my best efforts to summon up shallow smiles, my days crumbled like dry sand to the shore. This is grief: a collision of loss and life, where life fades as a casualty in the wreckage. The same can be said of all sorts of difficulties and suffering which leave us dislodged from normality. Some lives never recover from loss to lay claim to a new normal. These people remain wanderers, shadows in a life forever foreign to them.

I was in that place. Where I thought God was, he wasn't. What I thought he should be, I also found he wasn't. All that I thought about God was suddenly skewed. There were no clean lines of understanding or explanations which gave direction or comfort; only the disorienting sense of lostness existed in each thought, each breath, each day. The most discouraging thing about knowing that you are lost is the haunting awareness that, unless you are found, you will only continue to remain lost. The most frightening thing is that you might always be alone.

My formula was wrong. Faith, for me, was a merit badge, earned through effort given and beliefs held to. And this concoction of faith, measured in ease and happiness, served me well until I encountered a day far beyond my control. I had been the type of man whose "god is their belly," as Paul puts it in his letter to the church at Philippi (Philippians 3 v 19).

The image invoked by Paul in this verse is one of a man turned inward: one who is focused solely on creature comforts and whose ruling desire is tuned not to eternal life but earthly security. This is a man thinking he is ascending to the heights of heaven, that he is the center of the universe, and his desires are what matter most in his universe. That is the path to becoming a stranger to what we most need: salvation. Salvation is traded for security.

I wanted what I desired more than I desired God. It was me at center stage, demanding attention and response. God was not enough, I thought, because what I wanted out of life was not what had happened. Instead, death had arrived, and it had laid claim to more than my wife. Death had claimed all that I thought was absolutely secure and out of its reach.

Perhaps something similar has occurred in your own life. You may know the pangs of grief that remain in the wake of a loved one's death, or maybe disappointment or loss has so cut into your life that you are left bankrupted of happiness and security. In every form of loss and in every level of suffering, you will come upon two possible routes. One leads to destruction. The other is the one that leads home again.

To connect this meaning to the image in Paul's letter to the Philippians, imagine a grief-stricken woman who is twisted inward, so that she is concentrated solely on all that she no longer has, on all that has been claimed from her life by death or loss. This is the fork where a path must be chosen. Quite simply, the first path leads us toward the absolute void, where hope is utterly absent. The other path is a life-giving way through suffering. It is the path we choose each time we remember, even in the deepest of suffering, that "our citizenship is in heaven, and from it we await a Savior, the Lord Jesus Christ, who will transform our lowly body to be like his glorious body, by the power that enables him even to subject all things to himself" (Philippians 3 v 20-21). If we follow the continuation of the apostle's thoughts, we discover the profound knowledge that there is no end and endless joy for those whose hearts belong to a kingdom everlasting.

A common reaction when we experience loss is to retreat inward in an attempt to escape—but this only means we wrap our roots around temporal things, and elevate our feelings to the status of a god who dictates our actions and keeps us functioning as victims. One way or another, for better or worse, suffering plays a formative role in life. And so when we experience loss, we can find an opportunity. Suffering holds the potential to awaken us to life much larger than our own. Through suffering, God calls us out of our own little lives and their dreams and hopes and concerns, to transcend earthly things and know him. When we walk through suffering, we can discover immeasurable amounts of grace to withstand all difficulties in life. As Paul says in his letter to the believers in Rome:

> *Through him we have also obtained access by faith*
> *into this grace in which we stand, and we rejoice*
> *in hope of the glory of God. Not only that, but we*
> *rejoice in our sufferings, knowing that suffering*
> *produces endurance, and endurance produces*
> *character, and character produces hope, and hope*
> *does not put us to shame, because God's love has been*
> *poured into our hearts through the Holy Spirit who*
> *has been given to us. (Romans 5 v 2-5)*

Here is a plan for times when things go badly awry and suffering comes into our lives; here is a way of endurance. God is attentive and active in the details of our lives—even and especially in our difficulties and sufferings. When we know what God is working for in our trials, we find sufficient consolation for the swelling emotions pushing us adrift. God is enough. God is constant. God is present.

STRONG TO STAND WHEN LIFE COMES APART

Whether your grief has aged years after loss or is still in its early rawness, the invitation to follow God through pain and suffering stands. Only in traveling with him through our suffering can we ever find lasting fulfillment and discover a new normal where we find home again. Nothing drives the quest of pilgrimage quite like hope preserved. The absolute beauty of the Christian faith is not that its people move through life unscathed, but rather that we weaklings and wanderers are made strong to stand even when life comes apart right beneath our feet. Christ himself knows well the heaviness of this life. And it is he who bridged the schism caused by sin to make a direct path for you to walk home to God. Yes, friend—suffering is a part of our reality, but if you are a child of God, you have been made more than a conqueror in Christ Jesus (Romans 8 v 37). There is a great strength inside you: not generated within you but given to you by God. Take this for your journey: in each overwhelming moment, Christ has already paid your passage. There is not a single moment in this life that need crush you. Given the work of Jesus, given the certain hope of eternity with him, even death itself has lost its ultimate sting. This is truth. This is hope.

So we fix our eyes upon and dig our heels into the promise of a completed story, one beautifully redeemed and won through the gift of God in Christ. A day does exist when all wrongs will be righted, and every knot of your life will be straightened. That day will come. Until then, we hang on. We trust. Allow him to shape hope in your mind and heart. Realize that death, and all that it claims, is finite and momentary. Bathe your thoughts in God's word. Renew your mind in his promises.

In the convergence of two worlds—this one and God's kingdom to come—it is easy to lose our way amid suffering. Our hearts are prone to wander away and follow wherever emotion might lead. All we must do—though it is easier to write than to live out—is turn our eyes away from our hurt and the nagging belief that a dead end has been reached, and onto the kingdom that Christ died to open and will return to bring in all its fullness.

"Take this for your journey: in each overwhelming moment, Christ has already paid your passage."

#JOYINTHESORROW

This kingdom, God's kingdom, is "already but not yet." We live in a world of sin and suffering, yet we also belong to a kingdom where all debts and pain have been settled. What does this mean for our present suffering? It means that Christ has established the kingdom, but its ultimate reality is still to come. So there is comfort for us now, and for us as we look ahead, for we have a hope that is of far greater value than mere wishing. Our hope is not hung upon a star or a desperate prayer released into the stratosphere. Our hope is rooted in a kingdom already established through the death and resurrection of Jesus:

> ... a living hope through the resurrection of Jesus
> Christ from the dead ... an inheritance that is
> imperishable, undefiled, and unfading, kept in
> heaven for you, who by God's power are being
> guarded through faith for a salvation ready to
> be revealed in the last time. In this you rejoice,
> though now for a little while, if necessary, you have
> been grieved by various trials, so that the tested
> genuineness of your faith—more precious than gold
> that perishes though it is tested by fire—may be
> found to result in praise and glory and honor at the
> revelation of Jesus Christ. (1 Peter 1 v 3-7)

While we must live in the here and now, and though we are "grieved by various trials," we also are secure in the already-not-yet nature of God's kingdom. His power is guarding us as we walk towards our future.

Hope inverts reality and aligns our vision to see difficult circumstances from a "kingdom perspective" as we follow Christ. There will be heartbreak, yes, but hope remains in our hearts. Sometimes there are no answers in this day. But if you will allow, your hanging questions can serve to lead you deeper into hope's resurrecting hold. Lift your eyes higher than looking into your heart, beyond all that you knew or thought you knew, and further than any strength your own hands can gather. Look to God, and you can glimpse hope. Loss has brought you to this place, and loss can undo you here—but it need not. Even as everything stinks of sorrow and hurt, lift your eyes to Christ and his kingdom, and you'll start to sense the beginnings of hope. When the bottom fell out below my feet and the loss of Marianne tempted me to raise my fist in protest, it was hope which I stood on. We are pilgrims, led by the hope of a new day, journeying another step with him who guards us and watches over our lives, even now in loss, even now when we simply don't understand.

Teach your heart to sing a new song amid the tears and despair. Psalms 120 – 134 are often referred to as Songs of Ascent and as pilgrim songs. Scholars and historians have different views on the origins of this collection of songs, but common to all fifteen psalms is the sentiment of hopefulness, rooted in remembering all that the Lord has done and will do. Take the opening lines of Psalm 121 as an example:

> *I lift up my eyes to the hills.*
>   *From where does my help come?*
> *My help comes from the* LORD,
>   *who made heaven and earth.*
> *He will not let your foot be moved;*
>   *he who keeps you will not slumber. (v 1-3)*

These psalms are written to remind us of all that we have in God and call us back to hope and joy in difficult moments. Place them in your heart. The journey is not easy, but you will never be alone. We have an ever-present hope ready to help in our time of need.

FINDING TRUE NORTH AGAIN

Most of us do not live a life that seems to require God much in our day-to-day. This was my life: manageable and undisturbed. For the little that was outside of my comfort, I made humble petition. Whether I received what I needed or not was not of much consequence, because the impact of my requests was marginal to the quality of my life. My life was not out of control. Quite the opposite, in fact. And in this I had rooted my hope and trust.

Then came that day when, in one passing moment, the worst thing that could go wrong did.

The heavens grew silent. The earth pulled, and my life split wide. Suddenly, I was a stranger to the life of ease and comfort that I once knew. I lost my wife. My little daughters lost their mother. Nothing could still the quaking within our chests. This was our new life, one shrouded in tears and pain, void of hope or the ability to recognize much of anything besides suffering.

For me, the most disorienting realization was just how foreign I felt in my own life. Perhaps you too feel this in your own suffering. All who have met suffering know such disorientation. Just like a traveler who suddenly finds themselves lost, a reorientation is required for the way to be found again. True north must be established by a truth that is truer than present circumstances. As a magnetic compass is distorted through atmospheric anomalies, so too is our way in life distorted by suffering. It is a mistake to look to our circumstances as a gauge of and guide to our way. That is how we lose our way and circle with the spinning needle of our compass, back toward our pain.

There is a truer line for us to rely on.

His name is Jesus Christ.

As we journey through life, it is all too easy to grow accustomed to handling life and meeting our needs by our own effort. In a functional sense that gains traction with each manageable day, we grow into little gods. The passing days attest to our "divine ascent." That is, until we arrive at a day when we cannot find passage. When we are there at the end of our ability and resources, we arrive at the realization that we are lost and little in life. And it is precisely at this point that we discover again that we are, it turns out, not God.

But Christ is God, and he enters our swirling mess of circumstances and lifts us from our falling and faltering to lead us through. All we must do is follow. All we must ever do is follow. What Christ knows—because he has made it so—is that death can never fully have what it does not forever own. And so we follow Christ not only to death, but through it. In this way, death was a door that Marianne journeyed through: a door that opened to eternity. Following her death, my path stretched out into the suffering of loss—but my destination never changed. I shall walk through that same door one day, and I too will see my Savior's face one day.

In the grief-stricken moments of life following loss, you will feel the disorientation of life undone, and you will float through days as someone who suddenly does not fit into the life you once knew, and does not fit into life as it is now. This is normal. It is OK to not be OK and to not know how you will find normal again. If you allow him, Christ will lead you. And perhaps the greatest treasure of all, veiled in pain and heartache, will be the true you that emerges in Christ's shadow. Only in God do our hearts find the courage to leave behind what was, as it was, and to set out into the new day where, despite the shifting circumstances of life, hope abounds: both in the here and now, and in the eternity to come.

January 15, 2010

Let me update you a little bit. We are finishing out week three of radiation—this is a six-week intensive course, so radiation five days a week, chemo seven days a week. So far, praise God, we've seen little to no side effects. I did start losing my hair and so we buzzed that down, so now you can see the scar where they went into the surgery and removed the tumor. But I'm really recovered fully from the surgery and now no side effects from the chemotherapy, which is what we asked for and we continue to ask the Lord for. So we're doing well, feeling strong, the family's doing well, the kids are handling everything—asking great questions and praying great prayers. It's been everything we've asked for from the Lord in regards to just strength and being able to get back to some sense of normalcy. So we're really grateful for that.

The next couple of weeks are going to be key—the fatigue and the tiredness is an accumulative process and so the first three weeks you might do great; then the last three weeks are when it's supposed to get difficult, and that begins for us Monday.

Lauren and I are reading through Richard Sibbes' "The Bruised Reed," and we thought this was a great quote:

> *"After conversion we need bruising so that reeds may know themselves to be reeds and not oaks. Even reeds need bruising, by reason of the remainder of pride in our nature, and to let us see that we live by mercy.*

Such bruising may help weaker Christians not to be too much discouraged, when they see stronger ones shaken and bruised. Thus Peter was bruised when he wept bitterly. This reed, till he met with this bruise, had more wind in him than pith when he said, 'Though all forsake thee I will not.' The people of God cannot be without these examples. The heroic deeds of those great worthies do not comfort the church so much as their falls and bruises do."

That quote, both to Lauren and to me, has been ministering, and one of the reasons we've tried so passionately for the last ten years to proclaim the Scriptures clearly in a way that could be grasped is so that in such a time as this, for me and for you—I mean I am not the only one hurting, I am not the only one suffering, I am for sure not the only one with cancer—we might be reminded of God's mercy even in this.

Just some prayer requests moving forward: the next three weeks are supposed to be medically difficult on me physically, and so if you could pray for that; and if you could pray for wisdom in regards to when I need to rest. When do I need to just stop and breathe and take a nap and not push through? That's always been a hard line for me, and it's a harder line now that I have to ask, "If I don't take this nap, does that mean I'm gonna be in the fetal position for the next 48 hours?" If you could pray for wisdom for me, that would be great. Continue to pray that God is killing all the cancer in my treatment and not the other parts of me, specifically in my brain. Our big prayer as a family has been that the radiation would target specifically the cancer cells and that the rest of the cells would be untouched. There's a lot of long-term side effects that come with radiation—some that you don't see until eight, nine, ten years later. So we are praying against those things and hoping against those things.

Continue to pray for my family—Lauren and Audrey and Reid and Norah. Everybody is doing real well, but we're ready for the next three weeks to be over. Lauren's done phenomenally, but continue to lift her up as she's carrying this in a different way than I'm carrying this—and so wisdom for her and insight for her. And then pray for Audrey, who's seven and who's old enough to understand and grasp and be concerned and be worried. We're praying for healing, praying that God would heal completely and miraculously, and that we'll be done with this.

At the end of the six weeks I get a month off, and then we'll take an MRI. We'll look at the MRI, and that becomes the baseline for the future. And then I have six months of chemo and after that party schedule, it'll be different. It won't be every day—it'll be five days a month, and then at the end of that six months we'll take a picture again, and then we'll know after that what the plan is.

So you can see we've got quite a run here. I love you more than you know—thanks for praying.

4. WE NAMED HER KATE

Joy in the Sorrow of a
Stillborn Daughter

Kyle Porter

As I slipped the neck of my shirt over my face and wet it with my tears, my friend Andrea, who stood in our hospital room, quietly slipped out to let my wife Jen and me have a few moments of peace. I'll never forget that moment. The poignancy of it. The magnitude of it.

I silently wept on the hospital-room couch, and I thanked the Lord for my friend Josh, who had just taken a lap with me around the hospital's exterior. I thanked the Lord for my kids, Jude and Hannah, who were blissfully unaware of what was happening. And I thanked the Lord for Jen, who sat on an expansive hospital bed covered in itchy sheets and caressed our lifeless baby, who lay silent and still inside her bulging belly.

More than a year before this moment, I had become obsessed with the concept of suffering. I don't exactly know why, or at least I didn't at the time. All I knew then is that the idea and all its tentacles were pressed into my soul the way a baker kneads dough before it rises. I ravenously gobbled up everything I could find, immersing myself in articles, podcasts and books about suffering.

It was a strange time. I was actively seeking out the depths of humanity and sifting around at the bottom of the well to see what I would find. My mission was not aimless. I wanted to know why humans suffered, and why a God called love would allow such a thing, and why he would, it seemed, so often not get in its way. The answers proved complex, of course; most biblical ideas are if you see them in their true context. But I came to understand a few things about the Lord and his people:

1. Suffering should be expected.
2. Suffering comes because this world has been broken by sin, but suffering can be redeemed and used for good by God.

The first point I knew conceptually. Any rational human being can plainly see that all humans suffer. We don't all suffer in the same ways, but we all suffer. From the wealthiest family to the poorest panhandler, no one can escape the brokenness of this world, no matter how virulently we war against it with our money, emotions, and quest for control.

The other theme I began to see develop is that, for the Christian, to suffer can be (and often is) good for the soul. It can lead us to see and experience the Lord in a way we never have. It is something that the Spirit can use to, as 2 Corinthians 3 v 18 says, transform us "into the same image [of Christ] from one degree of glory to another."

These are the truths that I absorbed intellectually for weeks and months. They prepared me well for the path I was about to walk. A path I never would have chosen.

NO HEARTBEAT

At 6:24 a.m. on a Monday morning in December I wrote these words in my journal: "I'm getting excited about baby

No. 3. Really excited. I finally read the birth book, and I realized how curious I am to find out the gender. I could not be more enthralled with that right now. I'm also hopeful that Jen's labor will be swift and steady."

I didn't know as I wrote those words that the baby we had looked forward to for eight months was already with Jesus, and had been for a while. The story is a familiar one to many. About an hour after that journal entry, Jen told me she hadn't felt the baby kick for a while, and she became concerned. She went to her midwife, who also became concerned. So we drove to the hospital, but the truth was we both already knew.

I don't know why we knew. We just knew. Deep in the part of our souls where life and death and hope and suffering get worked out, there was a finality to the situation. It was already finished, and now we had the monumental task of trying to sort through it all. It was like standing at the bottom of a mountain that you've been told to chisel into a pile of rocks.

"No heartbeat."

All of the emotions.

Jen was 36 weeks pregnant.

IN HER THERE IS NO ACHE

Our friends, family, and church were spectacularly gracious in the days that followed. The weight of losing a nearly full-term child was not ours alone to shoulder, which made tasting the nightmare that unfolded just about palatable.

The pastor John Piper once wrote that he "loves the ready tears of strong men." I love that. My friends came and held me, and we wept. Their wives came and held my wife, too. It was a spectacular outpouring of God's grace in giving us deep and enduring friendships. These friends with whom we had built up thousands of ordinary days bore a part of our burden through those not-at-all-ordinary days. I'm not sure how we would have moved forward without them and without their prayer. The Lord sustained us throughout. We certainly did not sustain ourselves.

For many Christians, myself included, faith has always come easy. There has been no real suffering. There has been no true pain. There have been few questions. There has really been no reason to not trust God and to not call ourselves Christians.

Now there was.

Now we knew unimaginable depths. The sorrow that flowed after our baby died was an unspeakable thing. My friend Nathan said that until that week, loving the Lord amid sorrow this deep was only a theory for most of us. The entire experience raised so many questions, not the least of which is why God, who is mightier than we can even understand, would allow a helpless, unborn baby to shut her eyes and never open them again. It is an idea with which I have warred.

Suffering is a result of sin. If you trace humanity back to Adam and Eve, it was sin that resulted in sickness and death (Genesis 3 v 14-19). It was sin that ruptured the ties that bound our eternity here on earth to a perfect God who would commune with us forever (Genesis 3 v 22-24). Sin has caused suffering. God sometimes halts our suffering—and how rarely we thank him for or even acknowledge this. But sometimes he does not.

When considering suffering, it is helpful to look at the way Jesus' life ended. God did not intervene in his own Son's bloody, grotesque death on the cross. Instead, he allowed his Son to suffer more than we ever will as he died in agony and bore the weight of our sin. Suffering serves a purpose beyond what we can see or understand.

The Lord even told Paul that suffering would be a necessity as he followed his suffering Savior (Acts 9 v 16). God can keep us from suffering, of course, because he is God. But often he doesn't, and he did not in our lives. Our child died, but only because God allowed this to happen. That is a bitter pill to swallow if your perspective does not align with Paul's in 2 Corinthians, where he says, "For this light momentary affliction is preparing for us an eternal weight of glory beyond all comparison" (2 Corinthians 4 v 17).

When we properly contextualize our lives in this world in relation to eternity, we remember the looming glory that awaits. I do not know why our daughter died—Ephesians 1 v 11 tells us that God "works all things according to the counsel of his will," to which I am not privy. That is OK. I don't want to be God. I just want to trust him. This verse helps me trust. It helps me understand why God might have allowed this suffering.

I find it comforting to remember that for our daughter there was no suffering. If we got to experience both heaven and earth and were given a choice where to be, we would all choose heaven. That is where the Lord placed her. That is where she is now. Some might even say that she gets to grow up in the kingdom. What a marvelous thought that is.

Life here on earth is often good, but it is a shadow of that which God's people will experience for the rest of time. There is a longing in us that she might have joined us here on earth, but in her there is no ache. There is no dismay. She saw Jesus before she saw us. She got something far better than we can imagine, and for that we were joyful even in our sorrow.

YES, US

The day after we found out about her death, we went in for the delivery. That day felt like 24 hours trying to contain 10 years' worth of life. Years later, I remember almost everything. At the time it felt like an avalanche, but so many of the moments from those hours in the hospital are etched into a layer of my mind and my heart that is reserved for the handful of days in our lives which are more extraordinary than the rest.

I remember very clearly Jen saying that morning, "God willing, this is the hardest day we'll ever go through." You always feel like you've emptied yourself of the emotion, and yet it just keeps coming. It is exhausting. Jen was monumental, though. Amid my mess of tears and sorrow, she was sturdy. She reflected the Lord and his eternal goodness. She was faithful, calm, and trusting.

Never have I been more confident that someone truly had been saved by Jesus and loved Jesus than I was of her that week. Our marriage had been pronounced five years earlier, but this experience seared it into my heart forever.

She eventually gave birth to our child. We named her Kate Noelle. Jen grabbed her out of the doctor's hands. *Oh, my baby, my baby. She's beautiful.*

The doctors and nurses left us. I held her body in my 30-year-old fingers and flooded the only outfit she would ever wear with my tears. There was a peace in our room for the rest of that day, but even then I found the bottom of my soul, and its agony was inescapable.

Our friend Andrea was there to help throughout the day, and she went with me to find my kids and my parents. The background of the hospital waiting room was a myriad of people and tears. I saw our pastor on his knees. "We had a girl," I told my mom. "She's so pretty."

We got to introduce Kate to her brother and adopted sister. We got to read and sing and pray as a family. We told them that Kate was going to live with Jesus. Hannah, who was two and a half, could not have been prouder. Jude gave some heavy-handed pat-pats to Kate, as he was prone to do. He had just turned two. They loved her as much as they love each other. Of all the griefs we had, the toughest was that they never got to bring her home.

They didn't understand, but someday they will, and we wanted to have photos and moments to point to, to remind them as appropriate as they get older. I told my friend Josh that I don't want to protect my kids from difficult things. I don't want them to know only good moments. I don't want them to see only our good side because they will be mightily disappointed when they grow up and when they leave home, both in us and by how the world actually works.

One of our greatest joys during the entire week was sharing these fleeting minutes as a family of five. Jen and I also got to spend a night in the hospital with our baby. I slept fitfully. Everyone in hospitals does. I held Kate close while Jen rested. It was a memorable time that I'm thankful we had. It was also a bittersweet night, knowing we'd never physically lay eyes on our daughter again.

Psalm 139 v 16 says the Lord has already numbered all our days:

> *Your eyes saw my unformed substance;*
> *in your book were written, every one of them,*
> *the days that were formed for me,*
> *when as yet there was none of them.*

I've received over 12,000 of these days thus far. Kate only received about 250. That seems unfair, but the Lord wasn't surprised when she passed away, just as he was not surprised when his own Son died on the cross, and just as he is not surprised when any of us breathe our last breath. No matter how many days we live on earth, God sovereignly reigns over every one of them.

We didn't want to cry out, "Why us?" too often or too long, when these circumstances are so common to so many.

Instead, we wanted to move toward "Yes us, and thank you to everyone else before us who has walked their path of pain with grace." Primarily we are thankful for Jesus himself, "who for the joy that was set before him endured the cross, despising the shame, and is seated at the right hand of the throne of God" (Hebrews 12 v 2).

There is a couple from our church, Ben and Ashley Barr, whose son Thomas had died in a similar fashion in the exact same hospital room just one week before. They had literally walked the path we walked, and they walked it well. We took great hope from such great faithfulness.

The next day we let Kate go. Jen put Kate in Andrea's arms. I told Jen her job was done and that she had done it well. That brought peace, and it was finished. We kissed Kate's face and whispered, "See you soon, sweet girl." It was all so devastating; I would be lying if I said it wasn't. Driving home from the hospital without a child is a sad and empty thing. All you want is to hear the thing most new parents are aiming to hush: a screaming child.

The Lord was good and wise throughout our suffering that week. He was good to allow this suffering because he knew we would get more of him than we ever had before. So even though I don't fully comprehend why Kate died on the day she died or how God works that "according to the counsel of his will," I understand now that there was a difficult but sweet truth that awaited us on the other side of her death. It is one that is tough to reconcile: we lost Kate, but we got more of God. As much as we longed for our daughter, we delighted in getting to be so near to the Lord.

A pastor named Dave Zuleger once observed this about suffering:

> *Suffering is one of the great instruments in God's*
> *hands to continue to reveal to us our dependence on*

him and our hope in him. God is good to give us the
greatest gift he can give us, which is more of himself,
and he's good however he chooses to deliver that gift.
(desiringgod.org/articles/can-a-good-god-bring-pain)

MORE OF HIM BECAUSE OF HER

We put James 1 v 17 on Kate's grave. It says that "every good gift and every perfect gift is from above, coming down from the Father of lights, with whom there is no variation or shadow due to change." Jen said it means our faith must not waver because God didn't change, and he didn't waver. We lost Kate, but we got so much of the Lord. Not in spite of, but because of, her.

There is tremendous mystery in suffering. Walking through it is somehow simultaneously both good and bad. Its badness is obvious; its goodness is less so.

I have often wondered if I love Jesus because I attribute my first-world privilege to his graciousness or if I actually love Jesus. Then your baby dies, and you get answers. We can truthfully say that the Lord was good before Kate died, and he was good after Kate died. He always was and always will be. His goodness—even as I knew he could have stopped this and begged that he would—was paramount to my joy during the most devastating week of my life.

It's hard to describe what I mean when I say we got more of God. That is an ambiguous thing, I realize. We all saw it on each other's faces, though. The Lord was near in our prayer, conversation, and worship. We all shared a lot of joy and peace during those days that was far from man-made. It was a sweet and deeply spiritual week—probably the most spiritual of our lives.

Life that week was so thick and so rich that it barely resembled all the other weeks I've experienced. And the goodness in all of this (and a sign of God's spectacular kindness to us) is that the only constant we knew that week was that God is always good, and his grace and love roll deeper than we will ever know. He is sufficient, but he is also beyond sufficient. He is good to give us more of himself, no matter what the circumstances are.

We rested for a day after we got home and went to the funeral home on a Thursday. There are only a handful of reasons why 30-year-olds walk into funeral homes, and all of them are tragic.

We ripped through the minutiae. It was surreal. Picking flowers for your baby's casket. Picking a casket for your baby. My gosh. We chose four white roses representing each member of our family to lay around Kate's casket for the memorial. Picking the burial plot destroyed me.

She would be buried next to Thomas Barr. She shared a delivery room with him. Now she shares a resting place. Jen found great joy in this.

One of the best moments of the week came as we wrapped up at the funeral home. It can be an awkward exchange for everyone involved, especially when you have to talk about the money. We got to the end, and I asked the man in the bow-tie how much we owed him.

"It was paid for," he said.

"Excuse me?" I replied.

"Yeah, your friend Josh took care of it."

It turned out that many friends and family had chipped in, and Josh had simply been the courier for the money. I still cry when I think about that.

MISERABLE AND SPECTACULAR

The memorial was another sweet reminder of the importance of gospel-centered community. Our friends and family gathered with us, and we worshiped. We sang about God's faithfulness. We sang about the poor and powerless. We sang about how it is well. The opening of that last song, written by a man who lost four daughters of his own, is spectacular.

> *When peace like a river, attendeth my way,*
> *When sorrows like sea billows roll,*
> *Whatever my lot, thou hast taught me to say:*
> *It is well, it is well, with my soul.*

Not only did we sing these words, but we also meant them. Our souls were hurting, but they were well. The Lord did not remove our agony, but he did meet us in it.

The burial on Saturday was the hardest part for me. We'd just been hugged and loved on by our closest friends with whom we got to worship and praise the Lord. After that time in the warm womb of our church ended, we were spit back into the chilly December weather and reminded of the long road that lay ahead. I picked up the casket out of the back of the car and carried it to the spot where our daughter will physically lay until Jesus returns.

The box and the hole in the ground and in my heart all felt so small. I kept wondering when I was going to wake up. Instead, I got down on my chest and lowered my six-pound child six feet into the ground. As everyone got into their cars and drove away, Jen and I knelt and wept over the soil.

We went back to the church, and I found one of those men I mentioned earlier. He held me again and told me things would never be the same for any of us, and he was right. We all parted ways that Saturday afternoon knowing that we had been with God. It felt both miserable and spectacular all at the same time.

On our way home from the memorial, Jen told me she felt like she'd never worshiped like she did at Kate's memorial. In our 30-plus years on Earth, we have almost exclusively known great gifts and a rich life. We have a good life.

We have tremendous friends, enjoy our work, and delight in our children. And yet, the most profound encounter we have ever had with the Lord came as a result of suffering. This thing I was desperate to escape was also my gateway to irrefutable joy.

A LIFETIME IN A WEEK

There was a finality to the end of that week that felt crushing. We knew our friends would walk with us for as long as we needed them to, but we also knew they have their own lives. Our families went back home. We went to church the next morning, on Sunday, and everyone filed in and listened to the sermon as if 24 hours earlier there hadn't been a funeral for a 36-week-old in that very room.

We never really found out why Kate died. She just did. There was no specific medical reason or theory. It could have been any number of reasons, but none of them particularly stood out. She seemed perfectly healthy for 36 consecutive weeks, and then she died.

I sat at my home-office desk on the Monday after the memorial and thought about the lifetime I'd lived in a week. Seven days that felt like seven years, and it would take many more months to unwind it all. The wake of suffering is always tremendously difficult. I read, thought, wrote, and listened a lot. Jen cried a lot. We didn't really know what to do. We stumbled through life—mostly OK, but sometimes just pretending to be OK and probably not doing that great of a job. And you know what? That was fine. Our friends and kids were fine with that. Grace abounded evermore.

The next few months were a blur of learning, mourning, and wondering. They were really hard, but they were also really good. Although the week of our loss was when we experienced the Lord, what followed as the future unfolded was that we saw him for who he really is.

We saw that God was good within that first week of this suffering, but we learned in the months thereafter that he was also wise. He was wise to use Kate's death to teach us what it means to worship the God who gives and takes away, and to remind us that our control is an illusion. And he was wise to prepare me for years and years leading up to these days, so that I might be ready to point many people to him. I am glad for a thousand normal days of pursuing and talking about the Lord with my friends and my wife that led to this.

The pastor and author Timothy Keller writes that…

> troubled times awaken [people] out of their haunted
> sleep of spiritual self-sufficiency into a serious search
> for the divine. … It is an exaggeration to say that no
> one finds God unless suffering comes into their lives—
> but it is not a big one.
>
> (Walking with God Through Pain
> and Suffering, page 5)

The mystery is that God very clearly allows his people to suffer (which is confounding), but there seems to always be a purpose. Sometimes I wonder if it is simply to reorient our souls to the seriousness of the reality of our lives, both now and for eternity. Amazingly, as a man the Son of God also "learned obedience through what he suffered" (Hebrews 5 v 8). We felt the weight of that verse the week Kate died, but we could not be bitter because Jesus also walked through suffering. He lived that life.

That doesn't mean this suffering is pain-free or without sorrow. Quite the opposite, really. 1 Corinthians 15 v 26 says, "The last enemy to be destroyed is death," and this will happen only when Jesus returns to reign again. Until then, we will often feel overwhelmed by the arrows in death's quiver.

Satan, the enemy of Christ and Christ's people and all that is good, loves the evil, sin, and general brokenness in our world that causes our suffering, and even more so when it might tear us from fellowship with Jesus Christ. But even as he purposes how to turn our hearts from God within heartbreaking circumstances, we can say what Joseph told his brothers, who had disowned and enslaved him: "You meant evil against me, but God meant it for good" (Genesis 50 v 20). God used Kate's life and death for his own glory, and to demonstrate his victory over Satan; and we were overjoyed to partake in what unfolded after she died.

LEARNING TO LONG FOR ETERNITY

My day job is as a sportswriter, so I knew from the moment we found out about her death that I would write about it in some way. Hundreds of thousands of people saw the article I wrote after she died, which was pretty unexpected. It took me days to respond to all the emails and texts I got. Notes from non-Christians, from atheists, from those who had struggled with infertility, and from those who had experienced the death of their own child. I was ill-prepared for it all, but God was wise within the suffering.

I believe that Kate, seated at the feet of Jesus in heaven, was delighted that her mist of a life helped advance the kingdom she is now a part of. God made us less dependent on ourselves while working out his own glory through the life of our child. If you are a Christian parent, this is what you get on your knees for daily, and we received it! Jen said it like this: "We couldn't have wanted anything more from her life if she had lived to be 100."

My friend Josh confessed amid many tears on the day Kate died that he'd never longed for eternity like he had on that day. I thought that was a compelling and honest confession, and one that I tearfully agreed with and tucked away. I've always found my relationship with an eventual new heaven and new earth a difficult one to navigate. It seems like a place I should long for more than I do. I know sin has twisted this world. And yet, I like it here. I really do. The writer C.S. Lewis would say I prefer making mud pies to enjoying constructing sandcastles.

That's not something I'm proud of. But it's also something I find is changing as the years wear on. The more of life I see, the more I long for the next one. I don't think this is a unique position. Because of Kate's life and death, my heart has turned even more. Eternity has taken its proper position within my heart because of that week. We have talked about it more. I long for a new heaven and redeemed new earth more. I see the mud pies for what they are, and I long for the sandcastles.

One of our prayers during this time of our lives was based on 1 Peter 1 v 6-8. My friends and I talk a lot about enduring to the end, and I've realized that suffering is one way that you begin to understand whether the "genuineness of your faith" will "result in praise and glory and honor at the revelation of Jesus Christ." Keller writes that "trials and troubles in life … will either make you or break you. But either way, you will not remain the same" (*Walking with God Through Pain and Suffering*, page 190). We certainly did not remain the same.

I think about Kate a lot. Nearly every day since she died. Putting a baby in the ground changes you. I don't know how it couldn't. I think about her most often when it's extremely hot or extremely cold, even though I am aware that neither of these temperatures materially affects her body. I think about her when I see our friends' kids who were born shortly before or after her. I hold them, and I wonder what it would be like to hold her.

"In the midst of our despair, not only was God good; he was even better than we had ever imagined."

#JOYINTHESORROW

Stories like this one never truly end. Kate's death will always be a marker in our lives. It has shaped and will shape our worldview forever. I hope you don't mistake what I'm saying when I talk of the joy of that time. I don't want to diminish loss. We lost a lot. We lost a child. But we also gained a lot. This is a bittersweet reality too complex for me to understand in full. I wanted God to be powerful in my eyes and revive my daughter. Instead, he was powerful in my heart and revived my soul. I have not been the same since that week.

David says in Psalm 22: "O my God, I cry by day, but you do not answer, and by night, but I find no rest. Yet you are holy…" (v 2-3). I love that line. *Yet you are holy.* There is so much I do not and will not ever understand about Kate's death. I cried out and asked that God would save Kate's life, and he did not. I cried out and asked that he would change my circumstance, and he did not. *Yet you are holy.*

That is what I learned about suffering. It's easy to call God good when we are thriving and the days are flying by, and we should call him good in these times and praise him for his grace and his generosity to us. Jen and I believed that God was good when we had two healthy kids and one on the way, and he was. We believe that God is good now, too, and he is.

And in the dark midst of it all—when we had two healthy kids and one who we were about to put underneath the ground—that's when the reality of God and his goodness hit us with an overwhelming veracity. That's when we realized that we don't love God because he gives us what we want or what we think we need. We love God because he is God, and he is worthy of our love. We found out that Psalm 34 v 18 is true: God is near to the brokenhearted. And in the midst of our despair, not only was God good; he was even better than we had ever imagined.

January 29, 2010

With two weeks left of chemo and radiation, last night was the first tough night I've had in the process so far—just kind of really nauseous, and then I woke up about 6:00am with a bad headache, and since I got up this morning, I have felt that I got hit by a truck. So it's been the first tough day, but I'm just praying, and I've got to do my last radiation treatment of this week, and then I get two days with no radiation, so that should help. After the next two weeks I get a month off, so I'm hoping to bounce back pretty quickly and just kind of trust the Lord with that.

February 4, 2010

Now we're just coming off what has been a tough week, a battle-fatigued week, pretty bad almost every day. This is like having a really bad flu that just won't go away—it doesn't matter how much you nap. But the good news is that we only have one week left—in fact on Tuesday I'll take my last two chemo pills that night, and Friday will be my last day of radiation. So I'm one week away from being done with this round, and then I get a month off to let the body recover.

I'm well aware that I am not the only one suffering right now—I'm not the only one hurting. I've got good friends out there that are battling cancer also. I think of

Michael Spencer, who's battling a pretty bad brain deal right now himself. On and on I could go, so I'm well aware that I'm not the only one hurting, well aware that I'm not the only one battling right now.

February 12, 2010

Now we've got five weeks off. March 15th is the big game—we'll take an MRI, and then we'll have a series of meetings with doctors. If it shows something, that's a negative thing. Then we'll start the six months of chemo, which is a completely different protocol than what I did in this first bit—it'll be five nights on, 23 nights off, and a higher dosage. So we'll do that, and then we'll take another MRI, and then that's the one that becomes the "How are we doing here?"

Let me end by just saying thank you, and for those of you who just have randomly called, randomly texted, randomly emailed. So many of you wrote in and just shared your stories with me—those are very encouraging to me. There are dozens if not hundreds of letters—it's gonna take me a year or two to get to them.

Thank you most of all for your prayers for me and my family. Last year Dr. John Piper asked me, had I ever felt the tangible weight of the prayers of the saints in a moment. At that time I don't know that I could have said yes. One of the things that has really changed in this season for us is that there have been times that we could feel we were being sustained and held up by the prayers of the saints. I can't thank you enough.

5. I KNOW. I UNDERSTAND. I'M HERE.

Joy in the Sorrow of a Broken Family and Breaking Bones

Erin Brindley

I remember the photo from our high-school newspaper: our classic piggyback pose. My sister, the slenderer of the two, on top, and me, the stockier twin, on bottom, both smiling.

"She's the brains, and I'm the mouth," I joked when people asked about the interplay of our identical-twinness. We attracted the stares of strangers—the double takes and the frequent chuckles of passersby who wanted to vote us into the next cheesy gum commercial. We were used to the attention that never went more than skin-deep. And we became familiar with our story read from the surface: well-behaved lookalikes poised for success—athletic accolades, a grade point average of perfection, and commendation from every comrade, coworker, and coach.

But my sister remembers our childhood through a different lens. Her earliest memories are eclipsed by pain. I remember gleeful adventures of climbing trees, riding bikes, tire swinging, hopscotching, lego constructing, pond splashing. She remembers these adventures, too, but with the internal echo of brain pain, migraines pounding louder than a voice that was silenced before it could assign words to her inner reality.

She couldn't speak up. They said children were to be seen and not heard. That was the generational curse that snaked its way into the young soul of a silent sufferer from her earliest days.

I remember the next time our classic piggyback pose reappeared. She does too. Neither of us has a photo, nor wants one. We were trail-running downhill. She tripped on a rock, heard a snap and fell. We remember that piggyback ride down the mountain: smiles supplanted by grimaces, she on top, me on the bottom, struggling as one down the mountain. I cracked a joke—a moment of levity to assuage the pain.

She remembers that deserted New England ER, the X-ray confirming an ankle fracture, the surgery that followed—one titanium plate, four horizontal screws, and two crutches.

In the agonizing days that followed, her thoughts ricocheted, the bullets of a different sort of brain pain. She journaled:

I vacillate, disequilibrated in more ways than one. Reality heaves; yet I breathe. So I go on, one right-footed step at a time. Head adheres to truth: give thanks in every circumstance; grateful acceptance stimulates healing. Less stress and more rest are the best bet. But as I writhe in the night, pain not dormant and me neither, eyes cry and soul, too. Reality heaves, cleaves, and I struggle to breathe. A rasping exhale, then the thought: Can I this body leave, inhale uninhaled, rest of life unlived?

The familiarity of fractures. A finger, a collarbone, a hip, three ribs, a shin. Just another accident? A vague explanation without comfort.

She remembers sophomore year in college. Nicknamed "the animal" in high school for her swimming stamina, she led with her head, determined in every way to quiet the cries on the inside, always striving. But they couldn't be silenced. She kept it up into college with athletic and academic prowess. But the cries on the inside haunted her: she was no invincible 20-something.

They said her bones were deteriorating, like those of a 90-year-old woman. But those bones were simply a mirror of a soul already crippled by silent cries.

SO SHE LEFT

Years earlier, as young teens, we had stood in our empty bedroom, a haven of belonging since early childhood but now an echoing tomb. Our belongings had been tossed into trash bags and hauled off to an unfamiliar rental duplex. Mom said, "I'm leaving; you're coming." Dad said nothing. Neither did we. Divorce was a dream; an attempt to disown the dysfunction. But in reality, that dream was only a delusion.

Over time, they'd made enemies of one another. Years of unvoiced frustrations, silences that bred confusion and resentment, and words left unsaid came together on the day anger and passivity collided. The door slammed in their faces: one storming her way out with daughters in tow and the other shut inside an empty house.

Both were victim and perpetrator all at once. Both were silent sufferers themselves. Unaware of the wiles of their own sin-bent hearts and the schemes of the deceiver who wants nothing more than to divide and destroy, both tried to hide their shame with blame.

The deceiver, that ancient serpent called the devil, preyed on anger and vulnerability with the empty whispers of material satisfaction, business success, a better life somewhere else with someone else. So Mom left, and the deceiver gloried in his triumph. Another man took the helm in her life, domineering, manipulative and cunning in his lures. The quiet daughter tried to speak up against the injustice. But the cacophony in the home was just too loud. So yet again, she internalized what she was told and shown: *Be quiet because it doesn't matter what you think. Don't rock the boat because that only makes things worse. Learn to speak up... but only when it's what we want to hear.*

It wasn't how it ought to be. It wasn't how anyone would have chosen it to be. But it was how it was: a collision of confusion, pain, sin, and enemy schemes.

The verbal explosions echoed inside the walls of our home for years until one final "Shut up!" won the day. Speaking up reaped crushing consequences, so my sister stopped trying. Now there was silence on the outside, but through the internal walls of a teenage mind tormented by the injustice and internalizing the irreconcilable, the clamor continued to reverberate: *the damage is done; there's no way out.*

THEY SAID IT WAS HER BONES

The emotional oppression corroded an already brittle physical foundation. They said it was her bones. And they said it was her fault. But it just didn't add up. She ate more than her peers. She never missed a meal. Yet why was she still so thin? Overfed yet malnourished—so malnourished that it was sucking her bones dry. Bones: the very structural integrity of her existence.

But did they ever ask her? Did they ever ask why? Did they ever probe her silence before casting blame?

In the muteness of the loneliness, she cried out to the darkness: *Will I make it to 30?*

She did. She remembers that year. Her own sabbath year. Revived with vision, on the sixth anniversary of her beginning a stint at an East Coast corporate publishing service, she said farewell to managing letters on a page and turned a new page of her own. She quit her job, packed up, moved out, and charted a course from one organic farm to the next to her destination out west, where she would begin her new realm of study in ancient healing, a journey catalyzed by her own health experience. And then, in the middle of the plans, a fateful interruption:

> *I'm trying to count and trust and remember—*
> *and not grieve, as I'm wont to do. Grieve this*
> *opportunity, the once-in-a-lifetime summer, mine*
> *for the partaking and rejoicing, firmly grasped, then*
> *thrashed in an instant, gone—forever. Ankle cracked*
> *and so did dream… Will it ever be mine again?*
> *Will I ever run and laugh and play? Or will another*
> *physical injury, or a series of self-inflicted mistakes,*
> *plague me until the end of my days? Can I endure the*
> *shame and pain of a body gifted whole and healthy*
> *from the womb that I've since misused and abused?*
> *I'm groping, remembering, and giving thanks—and*
> *stumbling only on self-loathing.*

Yet, entirely healthy from the womb she was not. Those who were there remember those fearful first few days. I nursed and slept like a contented newborn. She did not: somnolent, exhausted, refusing to eat, losing weight, quickly becoming the slenderer of the two.

They said she was fine. And soon she began to play the part. They saw a seemingly happy and healthy child. And for the most part, she was. But the tenuous foundation of her first few days, a less than ideal but preordained debut, would plague her in the coming years.

She learned to keep the pain inside until it found ways to scream so loudly that others noticed. They said many things over those years. Migraines. Tracheal tear. Heart arrhythmia. Osteoporosis. Vitamin D deficiency. Pituitary adenoma. Lyme. Chronic fatigue. Thyroid. What they didn't say: *We don't know.*

Instead, they said, *We can fix that. Take this. And that, too. It's in your head,* they added. *Here's a therapist.* They filled medical records with empty words. Not her words.

No definitive diagnosis came. There was no date to chart the linear path toward healing. Circles, cycles, relapses. Confusion, isolation, condemnation. And so she gyrated through otherwise normal life—stellar scholar, exemplary employee, reliable church volunteer—shrouded in silent suffering.

She remembers that sophomore year in college. They said she was too thin. They said it was all in her head. They said it was her fault. Swimming? No more. Summer serving in the national parks? Not happening. Fall studying abroad? Think again. They spoke over her, about her, made decisions for her, without her. Successful student, star athlete, loyal friend—none of it mattered. *Psychologically unstable,* they said. *We're calling the shots.* And they did. Another once-in-a-lifetime summer with plans thwarted and dreams cracked. Like punishment, they claimed the things she loved, a twisted toll for an affliction she neither created nor controlled. They said it was for her good, but for her it meant only blame, chains, shame. She heard accusation, felt suffocation, and tasted injustice's perpetuation. Here was a different scene, with different players, but the same old story: unheard, imprisoned with the irreconcilable, damage is done, no way out.

CAN'T I HIT REWIND?
Pain persisted in inexplicable cycles in the decade that followed: sometimes injury, sometimes accident, sometimes
undefinable disease. But one thing didn't change: even when
the pain subsided, the lies of self-inflicted condemnation
kept the wounds gaping.

She remembers when God gave her vision for that sabbath
year. A flight home after a tumultuous weekend away, a mi-
graine too incapacitating to ignore, a simple closing of her
eyes to seek solace in her own silence. And it was then that
she felt led to set aside a year of rest unto him—to resign her
position, embark on a sabbatical year, and study natural healing. She took the leap of faith, and hit the ground running.

Until, less than two months later, her literal leaping
landed her in the ER with that fractured ankle.

*If only, if only, if only! Can't I hit rewind, all the way
back to the click, the start of the cassette tape of my
misguided life?*

There was no rewind. But would there be moving forward?
Was this a sign that her decades of deterioration were still
continuing at a too-rapid rate? This was no simple ankle
fracture. This was a crack in a soul wearied by recurrent suffering and the painful void of answers.

Yet one other thing didn't change. God bridged her vola-
tile teenage years and the maladies and mishaps of her 20s.
Simple faith was gifted to a soul needy of resuscitation.

Rendered immobile, she retreated to reflection, seeking
the journey in the journaling.

*Romans 8. I practice verse 32: "He who did not spare
his own Son, but gave him up for us all—how will
he not also, along with him, graciously give us all*

good things?" Wait. It doesn't say that. There is no
"good": he will "graciously give us all things" [NIV].
No goodness attached. In fact, a few lines down Paul
mentions trouble, hardship, persecution, famine,
nakedness, danger, sword, famine. Whoa. That's not
a list of "good" things. Yet is it a list of "graciously
given" things? The unhealed fracture, these months of
daily stomachache, this interminable fatigue—these
are not good things. Graciously given? Perhaps. Ah,
the bodily life can be such agony sometimes.

It wasn't how it ought to be. It wasn't how she would have
chosen it to be. But it was how it was: that collision of confusion, pain, sin, and enemy schemes yet again.

Though this time, she heard the voice of Another speaking, the very One who spoke and the universe came to be. A
God who doesn't author evil, and who gave tender words of
comfort to Jerusalem, to his weary people:

God says that his people's hardship has ended, her "in-
iquity is pardoned," that "she has received from [his] hand
double for all her sins" (Isaiah 40 v 1).

God says that "the uneven ground shall become level, and
the rough places a plain ... And [his] glory ... shall be revealed" (v 4-5).

God says there will be a herald of good news, one to break
the silence: that he "comes with might ... [and] will tend his
flock like a shepherd; he will gather the lambs in his arms;
he will carry them in his bosom" (v 10-11).

God says to look up and see him, the incomparable Creator "who sits above the circle of the earth ... who stretches
out the heavens like a curtain, and spreads them like a tent
to dwell in" (v 22).

God says that "they who wait for the Lord shall renew
their strength; they shall mount up with wings like eagles;

they shall run and not be weary; they shall walk and not faint" (v 31).

God spoke those same living words to her, too, one who was weary and faint. But was his good news for this day, or for a redeemed future yet to come? Yes and yes, both at once. There would be a day when she would run and laugh and play again, yet this would only be a partial glimpse to the perfect fulfillment of God's promise in a future day. But today: waiting. Waiting for the Lord. And in the paradoxical silence of a soul crying to the Creator came… contentment. Not contentment based on answers to her agony, but the kind of peace that comes with praise.

Standing on two feet after two months of one-legged life, both feet firmly planted on pavement. How stable, how balanced, how unencumbered I feel! Though crutches still assist each step, I've begun to bear weight. I'm relearning bipedal movement, beginning at the beginning like a giddy toddler. Walking unaided still beyond my ability, I bask in the standing. Rooted. Grounded. Extending upward, a posture of praise.

GOOD IS WHAT HE DOES

A weary traveler redefined as a beholder and herald of good news, she finally landed out west three months later, with renewed strength and ears tuned to the voice of her Creator.

God said, "Let there be light," and there was (Genesis 1 v 3). God said, "Let the waters under the heavens be gathered," and they were (v 9). God said, "Let the earth sprout vegetation," and it did (v 11). God said, "Let the earth bring forth living creatures," and there they were (v 24). Good. Good. Good. Good. God said, "Let us make man in our image," and he did, male and female (Genesis 1 v 26-27). Very good.

God said, to paraphrase Psalm 139 v 15-16, *I know you inside and out, I know every bone in your body, I know every stage of your life, all of them prepared even before you lived one day.*

Very good.

There we are again. "Good."
It's hard to avoid, isn't it?
It's in the beginning, in the creation narrative, when there was only "I am" and no "we were." It features prominently, an expletive (in the sense of exclamatory) on repeat to fill the void. And it adds meaning. Meaning to what God does. Meaning to the no-longer void.
So why does every grade-school teacher on the planet try to beat it out of us? "Find a better word!" they say. When it's bred into the very fabric of our DNA? What's wrong with a simple four letters that's done the job, conveyed the portent, from the non-beginning beginning of time?
It isn't even four letters, actually. It's three, if you count the double "o" in the middle as one, Siamese twins perhaps, the duplicate manifestation of a single source, a single body. Separate them like two lenses of spectacles to help each eye see separately, or slide them together until they overlap completely. Become one. One magnifying glass to help see deeply.
And when you do that you get three letters.
God.
The protagonist. The magnifier. Who pulls apart the overlap to reveal the good.
God. And good. The actor. And the meaning behind the action. One inherent—embedded—in the other.

Yet what of her pain? God and good—inseparable. She knows that. God is the gracious Giver of all things. She knows that, too. So where's the good in the seemingly not-so-good?

She has been afflicted, perplexed, and struck down, but she has not been forsaken or destroyed (2 Corinthians 4 v 8-9). Instead, her life bears witness to the victory of Jesus with more vigor and vitality than a pain-free life could produce.

His life in her and his narrative written for her gave rise to a passion that couldn't have been born in any other way. Her pain, ordained by God, led her to a new vocation, a field in which there was little witness to the Creator. It led her to a fuller picture of God's mandate to those created in his image, to steward and cultivate his world, including pursuing the healing of the bodies of those who bear his image. It led her to a noble pursuit of extending healing to other silent sufferers. What has been harm and hardship from an earthly perspective, God has always purposed for good—for resilience, strength-building, faith-nurturing, for healing of herself and others.

THE GUILT OF THE OTHER TWIN

In this story, I feel more like an onlooker than a participant. Why did she get the double portion of pain? We've shared so much as twins, and yet some days it seems that she's taken the pain for the both of us: that she's had to learn the hard way while I've simply received the reward of lessons learned from her pain.

It's hard to watch someone you love suffer. What do you do when there's no easy explanation, no quick fix, no assurance that their physical reality will ever improve? And what do you do when you possess the very health you wish you could offer them?

As I look back on our younger years, I regret my insensitivity. I thought fixing the pain was the end goal. I shelled out advice with frequency, fervency, and impatience. I discredited the emotional trauma under the physical maladies. And most of the time, I forgot about the pain that plagued her because I didn't live with it myself.

I can remember those younger years with guilt. Did I contribute to her suffering in my self-focus that failed to bear a burden I was meant to shoulder? Could I have acknowledged the complexity with humility, rather than dispensed advice that seemed easy and obvious? Could I have embraced my role as so much more than an onlooker, and entered in as a confidante and companion—someone to accompany her on the journey with compassion rather than counsel that only compounded the condemnation? The temptation for regret can ensnare me as well: if only, if only, if only!

Yet the pressure I've felt to fix, save, and heal—that's a load Jesus invites me to bring to him and not to shoulder myself. His yoke is easy and his burden is light (Matthew 11 v 28-30). She doesn't need another savior in me when she already has the perfect one.

The suffering Servant who saved her soul as a high-school senior also came to heal the broken places and refashion what I thought I could fix. He brought a redemption more pervasive than anything I could have offered.

He says to her, and to me, *I was despised and rejected by men. I was a man of sorrows and acquainted with grief. I was smitten by God and afflicted. I was pierced. I was crushed. I was chastised. Oppressed. Cut off. Killed* (Isaiah 53 v 3-9). Jesus took the ultimate double portion of suffering that we all deserve, in order to give us the hope of eternity. His suffering was for all humanity. It wasn't how anyone would have chosen it to be—except God himself.

"The pressure I've felt to fix, save, and heal—that's a load Jesus invites me to bring to him and not to shoulder myself."

JOYINTHESORROW

We both are the recipients of healing, my sister and I: a healing born from our Savior's suffering. And we both are not merely onlookers but participants in a grand narrative—a narrative that brings solace to our souls even in brokenness, and then does so much more as it propels us out into this broken world to herald good news to a hurting humanity.

Eyes cry and soul, too. Reality heaves, cleaves, and I struggle to breathe. A rasping exhale, then the thought: Can I this body leave, inhale uninhaled, rest of life unlived?

God said to her question, as he has to the same question uttered by many others, *No.* But he also said, *I hear you. I see you. I love you.* He said the same to his very own Son:

In the days of his flesh, Jesus offered up prayers and supplications, with loud cries and tears, to him who was able to save him from death, and he was heard because of his reverence. (Hebrews 5 v 7)

God heard! Yet his deliverance wasn't from the pain: "For it was fitting that he, for whom and by whom all things exist, in bringing many sons to glory, should make the founder of their salvation perfect through suffering" (Hebrews 2 v 10). It was through his suffering that God delivered him, and us. It was through his suffering that God extended to us a gift more wonderful than relief from temporary agony: salvation.

So the founder of our salvation—the one acquainted with grief (Isaiah 53 v 3), sympathetic to our weaknesses and tempted in every way as we are (Hebrews 4 v 15)—speaks into the anguish: *I know. I understand. I'm here.* For her and many others there is no date, no diagnosis, no definitive course of action. Yet there is hope in a promised healing. True today for her soul. True forever for her entire being.

FINDING HER VOICE

Yet some days were just hard. Taunted by the refrain of her culture—*These are the best days of your life!*—she found freedom, alongside the psalmist, to wrestle with reality:

> *Is this achy lethargy just the beginning of the end? I don't mean to sound morbid or hypochondriac, but I can't escape this internal fear, which flares up as the occasional panic, that I messed up big time and there's no turning it around now. That somehow I denied myself that pivotal growth period and now my body's retaliating—and that it will continue to do so, condemn me for my amorphous, unwitting, yet life-altering mistake, until the end of my abbreviated days... Six months since the fracture... first it was the pain, searing, throbbing, unbearable at times. I would crawl up the stairs at night, in such agony that I wanted to avoid any more pressure to the afflicted limb. It was a pain that didn't subside. Month after month I waited for healing that didn't come...*

Whether it's chronic illness, unexplainable ailments, injustice, abuse, trauma, or tragedy, the silent sufferer knows those dark days. The onslaught of despondency. The suffocating nature of flashbacks, nightmares and triggers at every turn. The re-inflicted wound of every emotion and suffering experienced afresh.

They silently voice their own refrain: *My fault. I'm the only one. Too late. Damage is done. No way out. Always going to be like this. I deserve it. No one could love me if they knew this part of me. No one would understand if I told them.*

They silently hear others retort, *You're too much to handle. I don't know what to do with you. Maybe it was your fault. Maybe you didn't have enough faith.*

They shoulder the shame, blame, rejection, self-condemnation, hopelessness, and regret that aches for want of "edit, undo."

Mute.

Subjection to silence is captivity—a kind of captivity that Jesus came to liberate us from (Isaiah 61): healing and freedom for the captive. This feels unattainable for the silent sufferer. Yet the One who spoke creation into being can give voice to hope.

> *Finding my voice. A sine qua non to recovery and restoration, I've known for a long time. Yet perhaps the hardest of all. Even now, far removed from the smothered self-expression of my youth, I find the road to acknowledged vocalization paved with false starts and setbacks...*
>
> *Do I have a voice in this dark world?*
>
> *The prospect of bringing parts of my story to the world, of uttering the heretofore unutterable—I find it both loathsome and potentially liberating. Silence is more comfortable—but is it ultimately redemptive? Is there more power in a difficult tale told than one suppressed unto death? Where is the boundary between blundering vulnerability—perhaps esteemed to the point of reckless divulging these days—and genuine freedom?*
>
> *Can I courageously—yet safely—release the stranglehold of silence?*

She voices victory over generational strongholds, enemy lies, and self-condemnation. Her trajectory isn't towards captivity but freedom. Her identity isn't sufferer but overcomer. Her future is not fixed by the past, even as she is shaped, refined, and sanctified by the echoes of it. When, in an attempt to make sense of her life, she rereads decades of journal entries, she's surprised by the pervasive tone: humble learning, resilience, even humor in the hardest times. The pages also chronicle friendships, laughter, joy, musings, work, labor of mind and hand unto the Lord. No, suffering isn't her identity. But it is indeed a catalyst for her passion.

Because she knows this journey toward healing hasn't been for her alone. Neither has her suffering been. Do you hear all creation groaning (Romans 8 v 22)? When she completed her degree as a health practitioner, she complemented her ancient studies with a certification in modern functional nutrition in order to apply the latest laboratory testing and technology to uncover hidden stressors in the body. She uncovered a host of her own: rampant autoimmunity and internal inflammatory responses to most foods on the planet. Self attacking self. *It's your fault,* they said. *It's your fault,* she heard. And her body responded to the insidious threat: immune cells attacking her own tissue, a self-fulfilling prophecy from years before.

What God designed for our good—food to fuel us in our call to cultivate—has become one very real source of her suffering. Our food supply tampered with, polluted and defiled by those charged with its care leaves their fellow habitants aching for want of true nourishment—many people are overfed yet malnourished.

Yet the physical maladies don't merely manifest themselves due to a contaminated creation. At times, the physical bears the wounds of internal torment. Physical, spiritual, mental, and emotional—all are inseparable in the body God has made. The grief and groanings, buried too deep for words, often cry out through the cells of the sufferer.

Her own cries propelled her into a vocation where she has a voice to revive the victims, sufferers, and weary sojourners like herself. She gives hope to the silent sufferers in our midst. She testifies through her work that glimpses of redemption are possible now: reversing generational curses, restoring familial relationships, resonating with people whose stories, like hers, aren't tidy or pain-free.

She is simply a wounded healer in the hands of the Wounded Healer himself, displaying him to the hurting, to those in desperate need of hope. While her pain runs deeper than the scars on her skin, so does the healing she offers in Jesus' name through her daily ministry to the body and soul as a health educator, practitioner, and coach; as a healing healer.

She speaks with silent sufferers whose pain doesn't fit neatly into a package of dates, diagnoses, or deaths. She speaks with empowerment for the whole person: body, mind, and soul. She speaks with testimony of God-sealed scars, imperfections, and injury that are no longer impediments to a life fully lived.

I watched this two-year-old girl tracing with her
tiny index finger the scar emblazoned on my skin.
She kept returning to it, fascinated, I suppose ...
But every so often she would pause her play, cease
her chatter, and toddle over to me, to my knees, just
below eye level, and to that fascinating scar. She
would extend her hand, and ever so gently, with a
stroke and not a poke, run her finger the course of
that ragged river in my skin. Then she would look
up at me, the wonder—why—poised between her
eyebrows.
I smiled, patted her hand, but did not acknowledge
her curiosity—left it suspended there in the furrowed

*brow and wide, probing eyes. And she, too innocent
for words, returned to play, resumed her chatter, the
question mark momentarily displaced by Mr. Bunny
or her number cubes, until unrelenting fascination
drew her back again.
No one else mentioned it. If they noticed, they didn't
let on. But the child did. She exposed my blemish
with uninhibited candor.
When do we lose our transparency? When does a
desire to conceal devour the childlike tendency to
reveal? When does the urgency to obscure, to shroud
in tacit silence and forced forgetfulness usurp the
clamor of curiosity, suffocate the how and the why
and the now what?
Blight does not escape the child's innocent gaze,
no matter how complete the mask, how clever the
disguise. She sees. She knows. And wants to know
more.
What's the reason? What's the remedy?
Oh that we might lay a gentle finger on our own
deeper stains and scars. And ask how and why and
now what. And not be afraid to answer.*

A PICTURE OF VICTORY

I pull out that old high-school newspaper photo. I smile
at the familiar faces smiling back at me. It really is a good
memory. The full picture of our teenage lives? No. But a
true picture nonetheless of the laughter, joy and friendship
woven throughout a narrative we can't change. It wasn't the
way we would have chosen it to be. And yet it was the way
God chose it to be. And God is good.

She may always be the slenderer of the two of us, unable to
escape the impact of a less-than-desirable birth scenario and

an arrested adolescence. Full healing this side of heaven may not be God's narrative for her story. But she is healthier now, healed of migraines by God-given common grace of discovering foods he created to nourish her physically, and by working out how to free herself from unnecessary sources of toxicity that had previously preyed on her malnourished body. She is more confident now: healed of crippling self-condemnation by the God-given gospel of Christ's suffering on her behalf, fueled by passion he ignited in the refiner's fire of her own suffering, and freed from the enemy's generational curse of silence that had preyed on her shamed soul.

Yes, that piggyback pose is still a good image for us. Not as a superficial cover-up for camouflaging pain, but rather as a display of victory. It is a declaration of strength that God has graciously given us in our weakness, a boast in the power of Christ on display (2 Corinthians 12 v 9-10). Teamed up as two from the womb, our story comes in a package of complementarity, not comparison. Brains and mouth together that give voice to hope heralded by the Healer. Hope for today, for both of us, into eternity.

February 19, 2010

Here's a big question that I'm getting so I'll just answer it. The problem with oligodendroglioma is that there's always a chance that it comes back—and so really the only way to know if God has healed me is to live for 30 years. Now the guys I've got to talk to who have battled cancer, one of the things they say over and over again is when they were diagnosed, when they were going through their treatment, they felt so near the Lord, so aware of their own mortality, so aware of their own weaknesses—and then what ends up happening is that it fades as they get healthy again, and they miss it. But for me it's never going to go, there'll always be that danger. And so I get to live the rest of my life with this being in my mind, and I'm singing spiritually now that this is a possibility that could come raging back any second. So I believe that God's healed me and I've got 30 to 40 years in me but the only way to find that out is to live that long and to keep taking MRIs. Now more than ever I understand what Paul meant when he said "Those are our plans, and I'm hoping, Lord willing, that I get there." I'm hopeful for things, knowing full well that my plans are my plans and his plans are what happens.

March 11, 2010

On Tuesday we had to do a funeral for Barry Keldi, who's one of our church planters, who died unexpectedly on Friday. He was 31; he left two children—Will, who's 3, and his daughter, Laila—and his wife, Charity. So if you would pray for them, that would bless me, to know that all of you are also praying for them.

6. CLINGING TO LIFE

Joy in the Sorrow of Anxiety, Addiction, Overdose, and Grief

Charity Ready

To cling to the word, we have to know the word.

When we suffer, we will either run to God or away from him. God wants us to run to him. He calls out to us through his word. God has given us the Bible to reveal himself to us and point us to our true hope in suffering—God the Son, Jesus.

I'd love to say that I've lived a life of faithfully clinging to God's word, running to him in every season. But to say that would simply be a lie. I'm much better at clinging to the dust of this world than to life found in his word. But, in seasons of suffering and grief, I've learned that healing and hope are found when I let go of the dust and cling to God. And it has been my Bible that reminds me of God's goodness and helps me loosen my grip on the things of this world, so that I can open my hands and gain so much more.

I grew up in a home with parents who sacrificially and faithfully loved the Lord. My earliest memories of my dad are of him teaching my Sunday-school classes or leading our family in Advent devotions around the kitchen table. His love for the Old Testament and the way he helped me see Jesus in its narratives helped me understand the story of Scripture, and how God was faithfully and generously working all things for our good and his glory. I cannot think of my mom without picturing her sitting on the couch each morning, reading her Bible before she started her day. Her consistency in running to the Scriptures, on good days and bad, modeled for me where truth, hope, and joy were truly found. God was adored and the Bible cherished in my home, growing up. This was a precious gift to me. The Lord used it to capture my heart for him at a young age. And because of the way my parents and the local church discipled me in the word of God, my knowledge of the Scriptures is strong.

As I became an adult and moved away to college, and later got married, my love for the word of God birthed in me a desire to teach the Bible to others. I began teaching children and women's Bible studies. I learned how to study the Bible for myself and how to look for patterns and themes. And I learned how to share what I was learning with others in simple ways that were easy to remember.

In the early days of The Village Church, we ran six services every weekend. For a while I taught in every service of our Elementary Ministry, which meant I was teaching the attributes of God five times. Those attributes were etched so deeply in my heart—the magnitude of God's sovereignty and eternality, the beauty of his generosity and goodness, the comfort of him as refuge. All of these truths helped shape my understanding of who God was.

And as I began having children, I taught them the Bible. Joshua 22 v 5 was being played out in my life: we were determined "to love the LORD [our] God, and to walk in all his ways and to keep his commandments and to cling to him and serve him with all [our] heart and with all [our] soul."

God used my childhood of learning and the teaching he allowed me to do to etch his word deep into my heart. But it would take an extended season of suffering for me to learn to really cling to God, and not just the things of God.

Because then my husband planted a church.

CLINGING TO DUST

Planting a church was something Barry had felt called to do since before I met him. We had originally planned to move across the country to plant, but the rapidly-failing health of his mom, who had lung cancer, and an opportunity that presented itself locally led us to plant just 30 minutes from where we had been doing life and ministry since we had gotten married. While this provided the opportunity to stay in an area where we had history and relationships, I think it also masked the reality that we were entering the loneliest and most vulnerable season of life we had ever been in.

For my husband, the people of God, rather than God himself, became the center of his life. It was as though the Great Commission—to go and make disciples (Matthew 28 v 19-20)—became more important to us than the Great Commandment—to love God with all we had (Matthew 22 v 37-38). Barry's good desire to see sinners reconciled to God and a healthy church established in our area became primary over loving God and pursuing righteousness in his own life. Without us really noticing, he began clinging to something that was temporary and would never satisfy. The church's successes and failures came to define him. It was where his identity was found.

In an effort to be a good pastor, he spent lots of time with his people. He was involved in their joys and sorrows. He walked with them as they put sin to death and strove for righteousness. But in his caring for others, he did not allow others into his life to care for him. We had no authentic community and no real accountability. Barry was afraid to appear weak, and he was afraid of being hurt or rejected. He struggled with anxiety and anger, which led to a pretty severe sleeping disorder.

I, too, began to allow my identity to be found in the church and in being Barry's wife. I believed the lie that we had to be careful, very careful, about who we really let into our lives. I believed that it was our job to care for others, but that we didn't need anyone to care for us. When conflict or struggle arose, we turned to each other to solve the problem or strategize, instead of turning to God in prayer and asking other believers to walk with us. When we were downcast or afraid, we looked to one another for comfort or to be each other's safety, instead of looking to God. We cared for each other and depended on each other rather than God. And the fewer people we let into our lives, the safer we thought we were. We were trying to be each other's savior, and we were terrible at it.

Of course, none of this was said aloud. In fact, if it had been, I think we would have easily recognized that we were living a lie. But the problem took shape unnoticed over several years, and it was allowed to form and grow because we weren't in community in our church, and we were teaching the word to our church without applying it to our own lives.

I placed my hope and confidence in all of the wrong places. I placed my hope in dust: Barry, our church, and myself. But these were temporary, shallow, lacking, leading to death, not life. I believed the lie that we were good. But we weren't good.

After 16 overwhelmingly difficult months of sickness, Barry's mom passed away. Barry did not grieve her death but instead went right back to work. He felt guilty that taking care of her had taken so much of his time and energy away from the church. In his grief and guilt, his sleeping disorder escalated, and he developed a hidden addiction to prescription medicines. Meanwhile, I was struggling more and more with a debilitating anxiety that I was trying to control and hide. Life felt out of control and lonely. We were surrounded by people who loved us. I am confident they would have loved us in our addiction, anxiety, and mess. But we stayed hidden. And more than we hid from people, we hid from God. We were like Adam and Eve in the garden after they ate the forbidden fruit:

> *They sewed fig leaves together and made themselves loincloths. And they heard the sound of the LORD God walking in the garden in the cool of the day, and the man and his wife hid themselves from the presence of the LORD God among the trees of the garden.*
> *(Genesis 3 v 7-8)*

We, like they, were hiding from God, trying to hold everything together in a feeble attempt to cover our sin and shame.

"But the LORD God called to the man…" (Genesis 3 v 9), and he was calling to us, too, through the church and through his word. He was calling us to come out of hiding and into the light—to remember Jesus, who had rescued us from our sin. To depend on him instead of ourselves. God was calling.

Confess.

Repent.

Come to me.

"And the LORD God made for Adam and for his wife garments of skin and clothed them" (Genesis 3 v 21). God wanted to cover our shame, and help us in our struggles, with the truth of the gospel of Jesus Christ.

But we clung to the things of this world for identity, comfort, and security. We clung to dust. And the dust quickly failed us. Barry had to resign as pastor from the church we so dearly loved. The grief and humiliation of that resignation broke us both. I remember Barry reading a book exploring Jesus' parable about the prodigal son in Luke 15 in those weeks after he resigned. I hoped that in losing the church, just as with the prodigal son losing his inheritance, my husband would come to a place of honesty about the sin he had been living in and repent. I wanted him to run home to God, like the son in the parable did. I was desperate for it. I was absolutely terrified of what would happen if he did not.

Instead, he ran away from God. He continued to isolate and make excuses and self-medicate. He found comfort and relief in a pill bottle instead of the word that he had loved and preached.

CLINGING TO THE WORD

"My soul clings to the dust; give me life according to your word!" (Psalm 119 v 25). I finally recognized that I had been clinging to dust, and the dust was killing me, suffocating me with its lies and hopelessness. I was done with dust; I wanted life. I knew life was found in Jesus—he is the way, the truth and the life (John 14 v 6). I was his. But I needed to set my eyes and my heart on him.

God, in his overwhelming mercy and generosity toward me, began to draw me back into the word. Everything else had failed. I felt so much grief and so much fear and so much shame. And in the darkest moments of my life up to that point, I began to run back to the faithful God, whom I found again in the pages of my Bible.

My life seemed to be crashing down around me. I was unsure and afraid of everything: Who was my husband with this addiction? Who were our friends? How would we care for our family (which now included a 3-year-old and an infant)? How would we heal and rebuild? How was I supposed to hold everything together by myself? While there were no answers to all of the questions and devastation around me, I found peace. I found hope. I found life as I clung to the word. Late into the night and early in the morning, as the children slept, my life looked like Psalm 119 v 147-148:

> *I rise before dawn and cry for help;*
> *I hope in your words.*
> *My eyes are awake before the watches of the night,*
> *that I may meditate on your promise.*

In spending time in the word, I was remembering Jesus. I was remembering how he interacted with sinners like me— the poor, needy, sick, and broken:

> *Jesus went throughout all the cities and villages,*
> *teaching in their synagogues and proclaiming the*
> *gospel of the kingdom and healing every disease and*
> *every affliction. When he saw the crowds, he had*
> *compassion for them, because they were harassed and*
> *helpless. (Matthew 9 v 35-36)*

I was remembering the sacrifice he made to reconcile sinners to God the Father:

> *For if while we were enemies we were reconciled*
> *to God by the death of his Son, much more, now*
> *that we are reconciled, shall we be saved by his life.*
> *(Romans 5 v 10)*

I was remembering his call to come to him for rest and forgiveness:

Come to me, all who labor and are heavy laden, and
I will give you rest. (Matthew 11 v 28)

And in remembering the truth of Jesus, it became easy to
open my hands, letting go of the dust of this world and instead clinging to my Savior.

THE OVERDOSE

I wish I could say that everything began to be made right—
that Barry turned from addiction and found freedom. He
tried. With everything in him, he tried. But he tried in and
of himself. He still was not looking to God for healing and
forgiveness, but was trusting in his own efforts and strengths
to overcome sin.

The work God was doing in my heart, through the reading of his word, was not saving me from suffering. It was
preparing me for greater suffering to come. One March day,
five years after we had started that church, when he was already confused by taking an over-the-counter sleeping medicine, Barry found a bottle of sleeping pills he had hidden
and took a toxic dose. By the time we found him, his organs
had begun to fail.

That night in the ICU is mostly a blur. I don't remember
much. But I remember the moment that the nurse came and
got me and took me back to Barry. I remember the kindness
with which she spoke when she told me that he probably
wouldn't survive. I remember feeling shock, confusion. And
then I remember the moment the Holy Spirit spoke to my
heart in a way I had never experienced before. Jesus, the
night before his death, had promised his followers that "the
Helper, the Holy Spirit, whom the Father will send in my
name, he will teach you all things and bring to your remem-
brance all that I have said to you" (John 14 v 26). Just like
the disciples began to remember all that Jesus had taught

while here on earth and understand it after he ascended, the Spirit enabled me to remember and understand so much of what I had learned in God's word throughout my life.

I was with the psalmist: "My soul melts away for sorrow; strengthen me according to your word!" (Psalm 119 v 28). The truth of who God was began to flood through my mind. All of those verses read, meditated on, and taught—the Spirit brought them to mind to give me something to cling to. I didn't have to search through the pages of my Bible for truth; the truth of the Bible was in my heart and mind. Of great comfort was the truth that God exists outside of time. He was with me, with Barry, at work in that ICU room. But at the same time, he was there 72 hours from then, in the healing or death of my husband. And in the days, weeks, months, and years to come, in whatever happened. I didn't have to wait for him to act or catch up; he was ever-present and fully in charge of what would happen. Not only was God present and sovereign; he was providing perfectly for my needs. "He who did not spare his own Son but gave him up for us all, how will he not also with him graciously give us all things?" (Romans 8 v 32). He had already met our greatest need for salvation in Jesus. I could trust him to meet any other needs that came along. I was surrounded by death but God, in his infinite generosity, strengthened me and helped me cling to life.

Over the next three days, I read the word out loud over Barry. I hoped it would comfort him in his pain and bring peace to his soul. I read the word to myself in the middle of the night, when I was supposed to be sleeping but couldn't. I needed and wanted to be reminded of who God was in the midst of this suffering. I knew life was found in those pages of my Bible, and I was desperate for life.

But as I was clinging to life, my husband's physical life was quickly slipping away. It became very apparent that his

"There are no words
for the grief when a
spouse dies. Two have
become one and then,
suddenly, one is gone."

J O Y I N T H E S O R R O W

body would not recover from the damage inflicted upon it. There are no words for the grief that fills the soul when a spouse dies. Two have become one and built a life together, and then, suddenly, one is gone. The past was a memory. The present was overwhelming pain and sorrow. And the future was looming with uncertainty and loss in front of me. Death was here.

And so we gathered in that ICU room—family and friends—to say goodbye. Looking back, I am so grateful for the time. Time to pray. Time to weep. Time to speak love and forgiveness. Time to whisper Scripture in hope. Time to sing:

> *Turn your eyes upon Jesus.*
> *Look full in his wonderful face.*
> *And the things of earth will grow strangely dim,*
> *In the light of his glory and grace.*

As my husband went home to be with Jesus, I went home to be with our children. On the day Barry died, I not only faced the overwhelming grief of losing my spouse, but I also faced the overwhelming task of telling William, my 3-year-old, that his daddy had died. But again, strength and life were found in the truth of the Bible. For William, they were found in a children's Bible, *The Jesus Storybook Bible*. This book, that we read every night to talk about the story of God, was now used to guide us in the hardest moment of our lives. While not the Holy Scriptures, these words, written to communicate the gospel to children, helped me explain death and hope to William.

We read about the day Jesus was crucified—about what his body went through as it was hurt and nailed to the cross. We talked about how Jesus' body stopped working: his heart stopped beating; his lungs stopped breathing. He did not see or hear or think anymore. He died. We read about why Jesus died: to pay the punishment for sin and bring sinners to God. And then I explained that Daddy had died. Like Jesus, his body had stopped working. And because Daddy loved and trusted Jesus with his whole heart, Daddy got to be with Jesus in heaven. I explained that there's nothing better than getting to be with Jesus. Daddy would stay in heaven and not come back home. There was so much pain and sorrow in our conversation. There were so many tears. And yet, there was hope—hope in Christ. We would come back to the Bible every night. And so many nights were filled with tears and questions and grief. But in our grief, we continued to return together to where we could find life—the word of God.

Grief takes time—lots of time. In the days, weeks, and months after Barry's death, I found comfort and healing in the pages of my Bible. When I was surrounded by the consequences of death, these pages pointed me to life in Christ. So each night, in the very felt loneliness of my bed, I read the word. 1 Peter reminded me of where my hope was anchored: "Therefore let those who suffer according to God's will entrust their souls to a faithful Creator while doing good" (1 Peter 4 v 19). Psalm 116 helped me call out to the Lord and trust him in my distress: "I suffered distress and anguish. Then I called on the name of the LORD: O LORD, I pray, deliver my soul!" (Psalm 116 v 3-4). I read through the narrative of Joseph in Genesis 36 – 50 to help myself trust God when I did not understand what he was doing. And as I grew stronger, I went back to serving in children's ministry because I knew I needed to sit under the simple, clear teaching of the word while I also got to share it with others.

What I didn't know is that, once again, God was using what I was teaching children to prepare my heart for the next season of suffering I would face.

IN MY HEAD BUT NOT MY HEART

Nine months after Barry died and right after William turned 4, William was diagnosed with bone cancer. In the midst of trying to navigate and survive our first holiday season without Barry, we were also in and out of doctor's offices and the hospital, trying to find answers to a broken bone that had no reason for breaking and a mass in William's left knee. I'll never forget the morning of December 27, when the doctor looked at me and said the word "cancer."

It's a terrible word that no parent wants to hear. And for me, it felt like getting punched in the gut when I hadn't really gotten back up from the last hit. I knew the truth in my head. I knew God was good. I knew he was in charge of every cell in William's body. I knew his plans for us were perfect. I knew I should trust him. And I knew the importance of rooting myself in the word. But I also discovered I was believing some pretty big lies that needed to be uprooted with truth.

When moments of quiet came—when there was nothing to distract—the lie that I was being punished by God would rear its ugly head. "What have I done to deserve this?" "What do I have to do to make it stop?" "Surely this much suffering is a result of my sin." "Does the Lord even care that I am hurting so, so deeply?" These questions and accusations played in my head.

I knew, in my head, that they weren't true. God does not punish his children. The punishment God's children deserve was laid on Jesus on the cross. "Christ ... suffered once for sins, the righteous for the unrighteous, that he might bring us to God" (1 Peter 3 v 18). Yes, God will discipline his children because he loves them and wants to make them look more like Jesus—"he disciplines us for our good, that we may share his holiness" (Hebrews 12 v 10)—but there is no punishment left. I also knew, in my head, that I could not "be good enough" to protect myself and my children from suffering. Some suffering is the result of living in a fallen world, broken by sin. I knew that I could not make suffering stop. I had no control, and I hated it.

But I also knew that God saw William and me, in our pain, confusion, fear, and desperation. He saw it all. He cared. Deeply. And he would act perfectly. He would work this suffering for our good. But I had to trust him, with my heart. I had to trust what I knew, even when what I felt was tempting me to believe otherwise.

I had to learn to trust the word of God over my feelings. I had to remember that my feelings were confused and shaded by sin, while the word of God was true and trustworthy. Through prayer and meditation on Scripture, I learned to fight the lies of my emotions and fears with the truth of who God was and his perfect love for me, found in the pages of the word.

One day I was studying to teach a 1st grade class when my eyes fell on Luke 7 v 11-17. In my Bible, this passage of text is subtitled, "Jesus Raises a Widow's Son." Immediately, my heart stopped, and I felt an anger that surprised me. I didn't want to read the text. All I could think was "Why is the widow's son dead to begin with?!" There was an entitlement in me that whispered that I should not have to suffer anymore; I had suffered enough. I definitely did not want to read about a widow who lost a son. It seemed so wrong. It took me a week to actually read that passage of Scripture. Each night as I read my Bible, the Spirit would prompt me to read it, and I would stubbornly disobey. When I finally submitted, I read verse 13... and absolutely broke: "And when the Lord saw her, he had compassion on her..."

I needed to know that I was seen and loved by the Lord. He saw my pain. He saw my sorrow. He saw my fear. And he cared. With deep love and compassion, my God cared. And he would respond to me with love and compassion—

regardless of whether or not that meant healing for William or death. Despite my resistance, the Spirit had once more caused me to run to God—the God who saw me, and had compassion on me, just as he had had on that other widow.

William was rediagnosed a short time later. He did not have cancer. It would still take months of physical therapy for him to walk again, and years for the mass to shrink away. I'm not sure I'll ever really understand the medical side of what happened that winter. I've laid that down at the feet of Jesus and learned to make peace with the unknown. What I do know is that that season of suffering helped me root out and put to death lies I believed about God, and helped me continue to run to the word in confusion, anger, fear, pain, and rejoicing.

TOMORROW

You and I never stop needing the word of God. It's not just something that we run to in suffering. And reading it is not some task we check off our list each day or week. God's word is where we find Jesus. And in Jesus we find life. The Scriptures are our weapon against sin. They are our source of truth in a world that likes to deny truth's existence. They point us to Christ when the enemy wants us to run from God.

After eight years of being a widow and single mom, the Lord brought another man into our lives. A husband for me. A daddy for my children. A man who loves God. A man of integrity and patience. A man who can make me laugh until I cry, and smile each day in a way I had forgotten was even possible. A man who knows all of my scars and fears, and pushes me to Jesus in them all. And as if that wasn't generous enough, God then brought us new life as we welcomed our daughter into the world.

But even in a season of joy and abundance, the scars of suffering still need to be tended to by the word of God.

There are moments of panic, as I remember the pain of losing someone I love. There are significant fears of being deceived again. There are lies of the enemy that tell me I am unworthy of love. There are deep and unhealthy desires to guard my heart against future hurt, suffering, or vulnerability. That desire for control and protection are dust. These struggles creep in on hard days. They jump out at me randomly. But my husband is not my Savior. And life is not found in my family. It is found in Jesus alone. I am continuing to learn to go to the word of God for truth and strength when my flesh wants to cling to dust.

I'm still learning to pray the word of God. I'm still learning to slowly meditate on a small truth of who God is, over and over. I'm still learning to confess where I struggle to believe and live in light of those truths with others. I'm still learning to rejoice and praise God for who he is, so beautifully described in his word. I'm still learning to do more than just learn truth or teach truth. I'm still learning to make it a part of the minute-by-minute, hour-by-hour, daily discourse of my heart and mind.

The word of God is my treasure because it is the way the Spirit shows me Jesus and transforms me to be more like him (2 Corinthians 3 v 18). In seasons of joy and in seasons of sorrow and in seasons of both, the word of God has helped me turn from the dust of this world to life in Jesus. And what I love is this: tomorrow, I will find something in my Bible that will help me know God more deeply, to love and trust him more. Tomorrow, I will find what I need to keep me running to him, and not away from him. Until tomorrow is the day when my body becomes dust and I wake to see him face to face, for eternity.

March 16, 2010

So today we went in, and we had an MRI done for 40 minutes in the tube, and those scans turned out really, really, really well. So my brain and my head are healing very well. The swelling's gone down from the surgery. There was some concern during the surgery because of some signals (some discolorization) further back in my brain, towards things that matter like speech and memory and motor skills. I'd been in surgery for eight hours, and so Dr. Barnett didn't want to cut into those, knowing that it could affect my ability to speak and move—and so he didn't cut those, because though it didn't look right, it didn't quite look like tumor or cancerous cells.

So today in the MRI that signaling—which is either swelling from the surgery or it's oligodendroglioma—is still there, but it is shrunk; and that is really good news. Our neuro-oncologist was excited about the scans— she thought they looked great. So—and this is the only bad news of the day—it turns out that we're not going to do six months of chemotherapy; we're going to do a year of chemotherapy. The latest research shows that for a stage three oligodendroglioma the best thing to do would be 12 to 18 months to really eradicate and destroy it. And so we'll do it for a year, and then after a year we'll sit back down and see if we need to press on to 18 months, or are we done. So the plan is that we'll get our chemotherapy in the mail, which sounds funny!

I was honestly hoping just for the kind of miracle where I walk in and they say, "Man, we're done here. You're healed. Go home." But I'm grateful to the Lord and ecstatic that he's seen fit to give me more time, and that's what today gave me—that those cells didn't turn into what they were calling bad cancer. They haven't gone aggressive glioblastoma multiform. They haven't aggressively sought to kill me. The Lord has kept that at bay, and I'm unbelievably grateful. Thanks for praying. Thank you.

7. BEATING ON OUR FATHER'S CHEST

Joy in the Sorrow of a One-Year-Old's Death

Tedashii & Danielle Anderson

It hit like a hurricane. We didn't expect it. We could never have been ready.

THREE DAYS

Early one Thursday morning Danielle came into the room and woke me up to tell me that Chase, our second son, was not feeling well. He had a slight fever and was not acting like himself. This was not the news I wanted to hear, as I was scheduled to travel out of town that day to teach and perform at multiple events. As a hip-hop artist and a speaker, travel is a regular part of my life. I went to his room and picked him up. He was hot to the touch and fussy, so I knelt beside his crib and used my signature cradle-rocking method to calm him. It was always an easy excuse to kiss his chubby cheeks. We got him dressed, and Danielle took him to the emergency room.

After a few hours Danielle and Chase returned home while I was getting some quality daddy-son hang time with Jaden, our eldest child, who was three. All morning, with an anxious heart, I wrestled with whether I should stay or go, but we decided that because it was a short two-day trip and the doctor wasn't overly concerned, I would leave. I threw a lot of random clothes into a bag and rushed off to make my flight.

Friday morning found us again in the emergency room— Chase's temperature was even higher than the day before. We left with a prescription for medicine and a machine for breathing treatments. We got home, and I immediately started following a regimen to help him get healthy. He was lethargic and not acting like himself; I prayed for healing and invited lots of friends and family to do the same. My mom came over to help me. That night I slept in a bed next to Chase's crib, waking every few hours to check his temperature and give him liquids and medicine.

Saturday morning I woke up and stood on the balcony to pray. I called Danielle, and learned that Chase was acting like himself, cheerful and full of smiles. What a relief. He sounded so happy that I could literally hear him smiling, so I smiled. Chase just has that effect on you. I talked with Jaden and left to perform my closing set. From there it was off to the airport.

On the ride to the airport Danielle and I texted about my travel details and how the boys were doing. I arrived at check-in, got my ticket and headed to the gate. During boarding I was upgraded to first class, which was rare, so I gladly took my seat next to an older lady. We got to chatting, and I told her this was only my third time in first class. She said, "Third time's the charm" and laughed. I had no clue what that meant, but I figured it would be enough of a connection to share my faith or at least have a fun trip. We discussed faith, work, family, drinking, Texas BBQ, faith again, and more.

I laid Chase down for a nap around 10:00 am. About an hour later I went to wake him to give him water. I loved seeing him slowly open his eyes, annoyed that someone was waking him from his sleep.

He didn't open his eyes.

I leaned in close to his chest to see if I could hear breathing or hear a heartbeat, but my own heart was pounding so loudly that I couldn't tell if it was mine or his. I screamed for my mom. She grabbed him out of my arms and listened for a heartbeat, but couldn't hear one. She said his lips were cold. Terror began to settle into my gut, but I quickly pushed it aside—I needed to stay focused and alert so I could help my son. I ran him into the living room and started to perform CPR. Someone called 911. Someone else ran Jaden upstairs.

When the ambulance arrived I felt like a robot, going through motions, too terrified to let any of my fear settle. Barefoot, I followed the EMTs onto the ambulance. The ride to the hospital was terrible. Chase wasn't breathing. They couldn't find a heartbeat. I just kept praying for the Lord to revive him: "Let his heart beat. Let him breathe again." Knowing it had been a long time since oxygen had gotten to his brain, I prayed for strength to raise a brain-damaged son.

At the hospital we were rushed into a room. They laid Chase on a bed and continued their resuscitation attempts. At some point my mom joined me. We prayed as we looked on with horror at the scene in front of us.

At 12:17pm a lady came over and said, "I'm sorry."

In shock, I screamed and collapsed into my mom. I went over to the bed and rubbed Chase's head. I gave him a kiss. Before I was ready to leave the room, the lady began to usher us into the chapel, asking me questions about insurance and Chase's age. She asked if I'd like to call my pastor. I did.

I felt paralyzed. My mom reminded me that someone needed to call Tedashii. During all the terror of the morning, he had been on his flight home and was scheduled to land soon. No answer. I left a voicemail, urging him to call me back as soon as he landed.

I knew that when he called back it would be time for the worst phone call of my life.

As we landed my phone started to buzz. For some reason I didn't check it but figured it was Danielle telling me she was at the airport. Once we got closer to the gate, excited to be back home, I returned her call.

She picked up.

Danielle answered with a faint voice. I could tell she was not herself, and it seemed she was crying. In a split second my heart began to race. With a heaviness in her voice she sobbed aloud, "He didn't make it." Confusion set in. "What?" I asked, feeling my excitement slip away. "Who didn't make it?"

"Chase."

There was disbelief. Maybe I misheard. Maybe she wasn't finished speaking.

"What do you mean? He didn't make it? I thought everything was fine? I thought he was…"

Interrupting me, she cried out, "He's gone."

I was frozen. I couldn't move. All I could say was "Don't tell me that," over and over and over and over again. The rest of the conversation was a blur. I hung up.

When a plane lands, it's typically quiet. There's an unspoken rule that everyone and everything is near-silent.

I broke that rule.

Wailing, I began to hit the wall of the plane. The flight attendant rushed over in a panic. I could see people leaning forward to make sense of the commotion. The woman next to me was startled. She saw my tears, my agony; she calmed the flight attendant and began to pat my back, consoling me with the very words of faith I had previously shared with her.

No one moved.

I fought to regain my composure as best I could. Either out of fear or confusion, everyone allowed me to deplane first. In a thick fog of shock and grief, I somehow stumbled my way outside to meet my ride home.

I don't remember much about that call—just Tedashii saying over and over, "Don't tell me that. Don't tell me that."

Soon after, Pastor Beau met us at the hospital and drove me and my mom home. The ride was torture. I couldn't help thinking that I had arrived at that hospital a mom of two, and now I was a mom of one. My mind flashed to the ride home from the birth center, a year earlier, when Chase was born. It was such a beautiful ride. I was bringing Jaden's little brother home. Now, I was coming home from the hospital without Chase.

REUNITED

We reunited at home, breaking down in each other's arms with uncontrollable tears as we faced the loss of our one-year-old son. For Danielle, this was the first time she really gave in to her tears. It felt like she needed to wait on me to really cry. I felt the same way. I entered the house to a sea of faces but needed to find hers; when I did, broken, I collapsed in her arms. Chase was our son; his mom and dad needed to cry together.

We kept to ourselves that day, though the house slowly began to fill with family and friends who came to offer condolences, bring a meal, or simply cry. It was surreal. We didn't know what to do. Though surrounded by caring family and friends, we felt alone. No one in the house knew our pain. We needed to hear from someone who knew this pain. We needed someone who could tell us what to do.

Beau helped us set up a meeting with another family in the church that had suffered a similar loss three years before. We met with them the next morning. They offered some helpful yet terrifying encouragements. The wife reassured us that we were the parents of two sons, not one: a truly life-giving reminder. They told us to grieve together, if at all possible. They told us that a new normal was coming—we wouldn't have to like it, but we'd have to get used to it. They told us that people might come to know Jesus through the story of Chase. Honestly, at that moment we didn't care about souls being saved from hell. We wanted our son.

The next few days were a whirlwind. Visitors came and went—bringing meals, cleaning the house, offering to take Jaden to play. I went to meetings with Beau and other friends to plan Chase's funeral. Everything felt wrong, backwards. We weren't supposed to bury Chase; he was supposed to bury us. We were meant to see his first day but never his last.

It was hard to decide how we wanted to honor our son, but a traditional funeral just wasn't an option for Danielle. She couldn't stand the thought of a tiny casket standing front and center of the sanctuary. Eventually we agreed on a private viewing on Wednesday evening and a private burial on Thursday morning. We would have a celebration service Thursday afternoon, which those outside our innermost circle were welcome to attend.

I was glad Danielle didn't want the normal suggested service arrangements for our son; nothing about this was normal. Losing a child, picking a design for programs, choosing a burial plot; nothing about that was close to normal. The weight of things people were asking us to think about and decide on was too heavy to bear. Our pastor and close friends had to almost threaten me into setting a day and time for the services. It was all moving too fast. I felt rushed. Choosing felt final. I wasn't ready for that.

I hadn't seen Chase since leaving for that show the morning of the previous Thursday. I needed to see him, to hold him, to kiss him. So I did. Wednesday evening I arrived to the viewing earlier than anyone else. I told everyone it was to make sure everything was exactly as we wanted, but really I wanted to have my own private moment with Chase. In a frenzy of emotions, I entered the room alone to say goodbye.

CELEBRATING CHASE

The following morning, Thursday, March 28, we had the graveside service. The pastors shared hard yet comforting truths. Our friend and pastor, Adam, compared life to waiting in line at an amusement park. He said that Chase got to skip the line—Chase was experiencing the joy that we all longed for in our hearts. This was comforting. Much later on, we would read a line from John Piper that summed up what Adam had brought across that morning:

And he will thank you for giving him life. He will thank you for enduring the loss that he might have the reward sooner.

Chase got the reward sooner.

Pastor Matt spoke, and explained that though we are "afflicted in every way, [we are] not crushed" (2 Corinthians 4 v 8). We get to be confused and ask questions, but we are never driven to despair. We have hope.

Our worship leader and a vocalist from church played "Never Once" by Matt Redman. We cried through the entire song. This was the song Chase was born to, and now it was the song played on the day he would be buried. The song became bitter-sweet bookends to his life here.

There is something wrong with seeing the beginning and end of someone's life—with being so intimately aware of one person's journey from dust to dust. To quote Danielle, "I pushed him out at birth. I got to experience Chase coming from dust—from my body."

And that day, we knew our baby was going back to dust.

I didn't see it happen, and she didn't realize it had happened at the time, but at the end of the service, Danielle smiled. A quote we found later by Robert L. Dabney explains why:

> *As I stand by the little grave, and think of the poor*
> *ruined clay within, that was a few days ago so*
> *beautiful, my heart bleeds.*

This is the harsh sting of death.

The quote continues:

> *But as I ask, "Where is the soul whose beams gave*
> *that clay all its beauty and preciousness?" I triumph.*

This is the constant tension we live in.

Death makes us have a bleeding heart. There's something wrong with it. It wasn't part of God's original good creation. Death came as a result of sin. But God gives us a triumphant heart. We have confidence that Chase is safe in his arms. We triumph because we know we will see him again.

After the graveside service we headed to the church for what we, to this day, call Chase's celebration service—funeral still seems too ugly, too harsh. Beau spoke. He read 1 Thessalonians 4 v 13-14:

> *But we do not want you to be uninformed, brothers,*
> *about those who are asleep, that you may not grieve*

as others do who have no hope. For since we believe
that Jesus died and rose again, even so, through
Jesus, God will bring with him those who have fallen
asleep.

He reminded us that though we will grieve, and we should continue to give ourselves permission to grieve, we get to grieve as those who have hope.

He then shared some short "words from Mom" that Danielle gave him prior to the service to pass on. Her words were to build your house on the rock—an encouragement to believe that God is all that he says he is, and an encouragement to do work with the Lord now and beg him for help to believe his truth, about himself and us. She knew, she said through Beau, that there would be peace and comfort to be had if we leaned into this Rock of Ages, the God of all comfort. She didn't know how that peace would come and she didn't know what that comfort would look like in the midst of such excruciating pain, but she knew that God didn't lie.

I felt it necessary that we address the audience together. I took Danielle by the hand, and we made our way behind the podium at center stage.

I had spent most of the week pondering a quote by George Muller that I felt compelled to share. It helped me cling to two anchoring truths: that God was good and that he was sovereign. We didn't know why he had let this nightmare be a part of our story, but we knew, somehow, that our story didn't contradict or change his character. Everything changed for us on that Saturday. Everything, except the Lord. His goodness towards us did not change.

After the death of his wife, showing impressive courage in giving her eulogy, Muller said:

God was good in giving her to me as long as he did,
and God was good in taking her away.

What resolve! It was the kind of resolve I hoped to achieve.

Beyond that, I shared the joy we had to still be the proud parents of two boys; one still on earth and one who skipped the line to glory. I wanted to give people permission to talk and tell stories with us about the sweetest, cutest, slobberiest, most chubby-cheeked baby ever. He is real and still a part of our family, so it was OK to talk about him. And I needed them to witness two people, filled with the love of Jesus and simultaneously with tremendous sorrow, who were choosing to persevere.

After the service there was lots of noise—even some laughter.

And then the silence came.

NEW NORMAL

Family and friends went home. Life for them was getting back to normal. We were being forced to learn our "new normal." We had to get used to putting only one son to bed at night, strapping one son into a car seat, no longer changing diapers.

We hated it.

We had been forced into the school of suffering, and we weren't ready.

My initial response to loss was shock, and Danielle noticed when that turned to avoidance. Reminded by a friend that Satan would use even this to try and tear our family apart, we tried to grieve together. But I didn't know how to do that and endure the pain. So to cope, I'd run. Run from home, because painful memories were triggered there. Run from the sadness of looking at his pictures. Grief felt compounded when I would see Danielle weep uncontrollably—so I would run.

In contrast, Danielle was trying to lean in to what she called the "waves of sorrow" that hit often, choosing to engage with the pain. One month after Chase passed, she found out she was pregnant. This caused a lot of mixed emotions for the both of us—anger, fear, excitement, confusion. We didn't want another baby; we wanted Chase. But we would take this surprise gift, not really sure why God would give us another child in a season of such raw pain. Since she was pregnant, Danielle was advised to experience her emotions, rather than stuffing them down and avoiding how she felt, because it would be better for the baby.

When one spouse's comfort is avoidance and the other's is engagement, it's really hard to grieve together. We learned this difficult task was going to be an ongoing journey. There was no one-stop shop for healing or "quick fix" for instant relief, but rather a new normal that we would have to learn to walk through together.

There were good days of pursuing one another, walking with optimism, and fighting for moments of laughter and joy. And there were bad days, which seemed to outnumber the good, when it would be an absolute battle to not abandon all we held dear as we grasped for hope. Walking this unknown, bittersweet path—trying to move toward health with your spouse—never came easy. But through counseling, church community, and a day-by-day renewing of our commitment to God, we began the arduous trek toward health, hope, and healing together. Honestly, it's a journey we're still on.

In those weeks and months, our pain was fresh, raw, intense. There were triggers everywhere that would lead us into anger, sadness, and despair. Seeing a family at the park with two boys. Watching babies who were born around the same time as Chase get older. Waking up every day and despising the unwanted extra time that we had because we were no longer caring for a baby.

We miss him.

HURTING IN HOPE

We both began to think about heaven a lot more in that season. Now that our son was there, we wanted to know more. Initially, Jesus seemed a consolation prize. It was nice that he was there, but we longed for heaven because of Chase. Yet in our pursuit of understanding more of heaven, the beauty of Christ and what was to come began to be magnified. Our desire for heaven grew to be motivated by our longing for our Savior. And because of him, in heaven we would see our son again too.

As our hearts and minds began to consider heaven more in its fullness, we gained new lenses through which to see our present reality as well. We live in a fallen world. Brokenness and pain and sadness abound here because of sin. Somehow we'd forgotten that.

We had allowed ourselves to be lulled to sleep when it came to the reality of pain and suffering. We saw it as an unwanted interruption to the normal "business as usual" life of ease and comfort. The less blurred our vision became, the more we realized that pain and suffering are actually the norms in a fallen world. It was ease and comfort that were the welcome interruptions. We began to read Scripture with those new eyes and suddenly found the Bible shouting out the realities of a faithful God, who not only has a purpose within the pain but is a constant presence with those suffering.

C.S. Lewis said:

> *We can ignore even pleasure. But pain insists upon being attended to. God whispers to us in our*

pleasures, speaks in our conscience, but shouts in our
pains: it is his megaphone to rouse a deaf world.

God was shouting all right. He was shouting of his presence and goodness.

But we didn't want to know these truths, at least not through these means. Couldn't we have learned through some other scenario? Couldn't he have just taught us in the classroom, rather than on a field trip? The nineteenth-century pastor C.H. Spurgeon said, "I kiss the wave that throws me against the Rock of Ages." Thrown we were, and we fought to cling to that Rock, but we weren't kissing the wave. We hated the wave.

HIS GRACE IS SUFFICIENT

We used to pride ourselves on being strong. We weren't easily bothered by things. We thought we were strong because we easily handled the various circumstances that were sent our way—loved ones divorcing, job loss, conflict in relationships.

But then one day the Lord shattered our facade of strength. He gave us a circumstance that we could not handle—a situation which, if we were left alone in it, we could not make it through. We were face to face with the end of our strength.

We needed strength outside ourselves.

And—praise the Lord!—at the end of our strength was his. In 2 Corinthians 12 v 9-10, God reminded us that "my grace is sufficient for you, for my power is made perfect in weakness," and that we could therefore say, "When I am weak, then I am strong." There is no end to his strength. It is a constant that we have access to because his Spirit lives within. So with confidence, we can boldly proclaim that there's nothing we cannot face. Nothing we can't do. He's got us.

We also needed grace outside ourselves. We needed God's grace as pride and envy spilled out from us. Danielle looked at the health and food routines of other moms and thought, *Really, you feed your baby that? I breastfed my baby and fed him clean fruits and vegetables, and it's my baby that died?* She looked at the success of others and thought, *Oh good, you get to enjoy the fruits of your promotion. I get to mourn the loss of my baby.*

I began to resent people, and even God. None of my friends had to face this loss that had been laid on me. People I saw, who had done far worse things, didn't seem to suffer. A friend encouraged me to be constructive and not destructive—to not let those things drive me to a negative place. And though I heard her, I struggled to take her advice to heart. I was angry that any of this was part of my new normal.

I decided to lean in to what I felt by making music that could consider and communicate my reality. As I did, I realized that I had selfishly, yet naturally, wanted God to give me a pass. Like a get-out-of-jail-free card, I had wanted a get-out-of-suffering-free card that would have shielded me from things like this, because I deserved it. I had traveled the world sharing God's good news: preaching, doing missions, constantly trying to be a light. So this tragedy was supposed to be someone else's story, never mine, because I had earned a special pass. Somewhere along the line, I had fostered the idea that God would keep calamity at bay because I was "a child of God."

In the midst of our ugly thoughts being exposed, God's grace was sufficient. His grace covered our sin and revealed where our hearts were not like his. His grace forgave. His grace enabled us to confess and repent—often. He taught us not to dismiss how we felt but to be honest with him about it. And he reminded us of the greatest news, a beautiful

"This tragedy was supposed to be someone else's story. I had fostered the idea that God would keep calamity at bay because I was a 'child of God.'"

#JOYINTHESORROW

truth: that despite our internal ugliness, he hadn't left us, and he never would.

He was with us: in the pain, the sorrow, the confusion, the terror. Not only was his presence promised, but restoration was promised too:

> *And after you have suffered a little while, the God of all grace, who has called you to his eternal glory in Christ, will himself restore, confirm, strengthen, and establish you. (1 Peter 5 v 10)*

When we first read that verse, it was offensive. A "little while"? We were going to have to carry this pain, this burden, this absence for the rest of our lives. That's not little. That's a lifetime. But over time, we came to understand that in the grand scheme of eternity, our remaining forty, fifty, or sixty years truly was a little while. We had no idea how we would make it through our "little while," but we did know that Lamentations 3 v 22-23 promised us that...

> *the steadfast love of the LORD never ceases;*
> *his mercies never come to an end;*
> *they are new every morning;*
> *great is [his] faithfulness.*

So we fought to take it one day at a time. We fought to tell ourselves that his love wasn't stopping, wasn't going away. This was a truth not easily accepted. His love for us was present when Chase took his last breath. This nightmare had been sifted through his hand of love before he allowed it to touch us. Frustrating. Mind blowing.

So there we were, trapped in our "little while."

Trapped with new mercies.

Trapped in love.

We were broken and had nowhere else to turn. We were like sad and angry little children beating on our Father's chest as he held us in his lap.

So, we decided to wake up each day and remind ourselves that he loved us. We didn't believe it every time, but we tried. We tried to exhaust the new mercies of the day too. Some days there didn't seem to be enough. We went to bed exhausted and heartbroken, angry that all the pain we'd been through that day was just that—a day. But we knew there would be love and new mercies awaiting us in the morning. And over and over we went, day by day.

We've been living this one-day-at-a-time life for years now. The intensity of the pain has lightened, though there are times when grief comes crashing down like a tumultuous wave. In those moments, we remind ourselves that God is with us and Chase is with him, and we keep going through our "little while."

WE AREN'T OK, BUT...

The darkness has been thick.

We had no idea how dark the dark night of the soul could actually be. And, to be honest, we haven't made it through yet. We're honest when we say, "We're not OK; things aren't OK." We miss Chase every day. We miss him on Mother's Day, on Father's Day, at Christmas, at New Year. We miss him on his birthday, Jaden's birthday, Callen's birthday, Kai's birthday. We missed him on what could have been his first day of preschool, kindergarten, first grade. We miss him when we see four brothers from a different family playing at the park. We miss him when we miss him.

We aren't OK, but we are being mended, healed. We find ourselves on a long journey of grief and restoration, and we long for the day when our healing will be complete.

A year after we were thrust into this "little while," I released an album called "Below Paradise." On it, I wrote a song about Chase. The lament from the chorus still rings true:

> *You give and you take.*
> *Through it all, I will chase*
> *after your heart not your hand when my heart don't*
> *understand.*
> *I will go chasin' you, trust in you, hope in you—*
> *forever.*

We are hurt. We are human. We are his.

April 23, 2010

We just finished Round Two, Phase Two, which was the full-dose chemo—and unfortunately, the side-effects finally showed up. I was in Orlando teaching most of this week, and noticed while I was there that I was just kind of melancholy. I wasn't myself, I didn't really want to be around anybody, I kind of wanted just to stay in the hotel, and I started feeling—I don't know how to explain it—dark.

I flew home early—I spoke, ran offstage, got into the car, got to the airport early, and took an earlier flight home. Today was just a rough day in regards to the nausea, and I still had that kind of darkness on me. So I called my doctor and found out that one of the side effects of the treatment is depression. That's what I've been battling a lot, which is a strange feeling for me, and so the doctor kind of said, "OK, now we know how it'll manifest itself." So still no fatigue—praise God for that—but I had to coerce myself out of bed this morning and coerce myself into leaving the house for a little while, because I wanted to just stay in bed.

So that's a new feeling for me. I couldn't help but think of Spurgeon and how faithful he was to do all he did while he struggled. So it's been a very difficult week. It's been interesting to kind of run into a wall finally—but God's just as good as if it didn't happen at all, and as he was when we weren't struggling.

May 7, 2010

On Tuesday the eighteenth, at 8.30 in the morning, we go in for a pretty huge MRI. They're going to use perfusion, which is going to show blood flow in my brain. There's a little cloud that showed up a month or two ago in my MRI, and it is one of three things: it's scar tissue; it's swelling from the surgery and radiation; or it's oligodendroglioma trying to form another tumor in a pretty bad spot. Perfusion is going to show us what that is. So by one o'clock on the 18th, we'll have either really, really, really good news to celebrate, or really, really hard news to celebrate. So we appreciate your prayers for the sudden anxiety we're feeling about that scan. Thank you so much for your prayers. We love you guys more than you know, and I appreciate how you stand in the gap for me and my family. We have felt the Spirit's power in our lives manifest more and more as you guys have been so faithful to pray. So thank you.

8. NO NEED TO BE AFRAID

Joy in the Sorrow of Family Chaos, Illness, and Death

Anne Lincoln Holibaugh

I have very few memories before things were hard in our family. I know from pictures that the early years of my childhood were stable, safe, and full of life. I see that my parents loved each other and adored me, and that we did things together and seemed happy. But most of what I actually remember tells a different story.

I remember waking up for school when I was six or seven years old and overhearing my mom call into work. She didn't feel well and needed to take a day of vacation. Her tone told me something was wrong. That call happened again. And then again. Soon after came frequent doctor's visits, long waits at the drugstore for new prescriptions, and stays in the hospital. I didn't know it, but it was the beginning of my mom fading away.

I also remember coming home from school in my early elementary years and being told to go to my room while my parents talked in the kitchen. It was unusual for my dad to be home at that time of day, and I could tell something serious was happening. So, as a naturally curious kid, I snuck to within earshot of their conversation. My dad had lost his job. It wouldn't be the last time. I remember he cursed when he realized I was there listening. It scared me. That, too, would happen again. Many times.

SHAME AND FEAR

So began my family's descent into chaos. From that point, my upbringing became characterized by scarcity, sickness, fear, hiding, and shame. My mom was chronically ill and became increasingly unable to care for me or our home. Our roles gradually reversed, with me becoming her caregiver and assuming responsibilities disproportionate to both my age and place in our family.

The stress on my father and their marriage must have been tremendous. In and out of work, with a sick wife and a young daughter, I'm sure he felt out of control and afraid. His anger and our fear of it set the temperature of our home.

Dutifully, I took up my post as peacekeeper and protector. I was eager to please, eager to be perfect, doing whatever I could to avoid my dad getting upset or my mom being sad. I did my best to hold my world together with what felt like scotch tape and good grades. I began to hide behind my ability to perform, hoping that no one would be able to see the brokenness bulging from behind our front door. I felt such shame, and I was afraid of both people and the future.

I remember, even at a young age, creating contingency plans for any number of possible worst-case scenarios, the most dire being the death of one or both of my parents. They were getting older, and with my mom in and out of the hospital, it seemed like a terrible inevitability. And I needed to be ready for it. Otherwise, what would happen?

Who would make sure things were OK? Even though I knew our family was unhealthy and dysfunctional, I was terrified of not having one at all.

I remember spending hours on our front porch begging God not to let my parents die, bargaining with him for more time. I grew up with limited exposure to church and biblical teaching, but I remember knowing that God was real. And I guess I also thought of him as good, because I don't remember hesitating to talk to him, even before I put my trust in him or knew much about prayer.

Even when I became a Christian at 14, I couldn't have articulated much about the Lord or his word. But I believed, and I wanted to know him. Whatever he required of me I was eager to do. I was like a sponge, soaking up every bit of truth and teaching available. I experienced joy and peace in his presence, and I felt safe for the first time. Though I wouldn't understand the significance for several years, God had adopted me into his family, as a beloved child among many beloved children, completely covered and provided for perfectly.

I think it's easy for those who have been Christians for some time to forget the literal miracle that it is to be born again. God's power and love are astounding. In salvation, God not only brings his children out of what is bad but also into what is good. He "has delivered us from the domain of darkness"—the darkness and damnation of sin—"and transferred us to the kingdom of his beloved Son," as members of his loving, everlasting family (Colossians 1 v 13). Sometimes we can lose sight of that, especially when we're facing hardship, trauma, and trial. More significant than being delivered from difficult and dangerous circumstances is being delivered from the source of them—the sin that has broken the world and separated us from God.

"How could a loving
   God desire his glory
   such that he would let
   his children suffer?
   For me, this question
   was not hypothetical—
   it was deeply personal
   and urgent."

#JOYINTHESORROW

COULD GOD BE SOVEREIGN *AND* GOOD?

As I grew in my relationship with the Lord through my teenage years, things within my family grew more difficult. My mother's health continued to decline. The tension and disorder in our home only increased. I eventually left for college which, in one sense, was a relief. I welcomed the reprieve from the chaos. But I also carried a huge burden of guilt for leaving my parents. I felt like I was abandoning my mom to be cared for by a man who had grown to resent her deeply, and I was afraid that my dad would collapse under the stress.

It was during college that I was surrounded by Christian community and became part of a local church for the first time. I was still sponge-like as a young believer and was eager to learn about God and from his word. But as I grew in my faith, I struggled to reconcile the suffering I witnessed and experienced with what I was learning about God's sovereignty and goodness. God was unquestionably sovereign (Isaiah 40 v 22-24), unwaveringly good (Psalm 119 v 68), and fiercely committed to his glory (Isaiah 42 v 8). So why was the world so broken? And how could this all-powerful God desire all people to know him but not act to make that so? Those around me talked about God's sovereignty as a warm blanket for the soul, but it didn't feel like that for me. It felt mean. And confusing. It made him seem aloof—glorious, but uninvolved. To know that "God is in the heavens; he does all that he pleases" (Psalm 115 v 3) and yet be in so much pain led me to feel that it must surely not please or glorify God to hear my prayer and draw near. How could a good and loving God desire his glory above all things such that he would let his children suffer?

For me, that question and others like it were not hypothetical. They were deeply personal and urgent. While I was learning about God's sovereignty over all things, including suffering, I was also watching my mother waste away in both body and mind. Those two things did not make sense together. I vividly remember thinking that if her suffering was for God's glory, then I wanted nothing to do with it. I was deeply offended by even the idea that God could be doing anything good through this pain. I didn't yet understand the way God uses affliction to strengthen and sift the faith of his children, and how he glorifies himself in drawing near to the weak. I was still to learn that God hates death and the suffering of his children, even though he uses both to accomplish his will. I was hurting, angry, scared, and confused. I wanted to know what was true about God and trust him by faith, but I felt lost and totally alone.

This was my dark night of the soul.

In love, God let me feel the discomfort of my limited and (in some ways) incorrect understanding of him. While he did not lift me out of that wrestle immediately, he also didn't leave me to it forever. Psalm 145 promises that "the Lord upholds all who are falling and raises up all who are bowed down" (v 14), that he is "righteous in all his ways and kind in all his works," and that God is "near to all who call on him, to all who call on him in truth" (v 18). And I experienced this. Powerfully and tenderly, the Lord brought renewed assurance that, though there were things I could not and would not understand in the way I wanted to, he was good—righteous and kind—and he was with me. And that was enough. His presence and promise to be near were better and more beautiful than the removal of confusion or a painful circumstance, even when that painful circumstance was my mom's death.

THE LAST TIME I SAW HER

I remember the last time I saw her. I had come home for the weekend. Her body and mind were weak. She was a shadow of the woman I had once known: full of life, who loved music and beauty and being outside. I remember hugging her goodbye. I can see and feel that moment even now. Somehow I knew it was the last time I would see her, hug her, hear her voice. And I was right. Two days later, she passed away.

I wasn't there when she died.

I remember getting the phone call from my dad, frantic and reeling. I remember numbly packing a bag and driving home. I remember sitting quiet and confused as people planned a small service for her at the old church in East Texas where she had grown up. We sang "Rock of Ages." I spoke words about my mom and from 1 Corinthians 13, which was marked as her favorite passage in the Bible she had given me the first year I went to camp.

And then we all went home.

In many ways, my day-to-day life felt relatively unchanged after she passed. I wasn't devastated the way some might have expected. I wasn't left to suddenly figure out how to live without my mother's care and presence. In that way, I had lost my mom long before the day she died. Her life and spirit had ebbed away over the course of years. And she had watched me watch her fade away, unable to be the mother she had waited so long to be. I can't imagine what that was like for her. I know what it was like for me: it was awful. While I certainly didn't want my mom to die, I also didn't want her to suffer anymore.

Losing someone you love is never easy. Whether it happens suddenly or is anticipated at the end of a long illness, loss is loss. Death is devastating. That's because as those made in God's image, with and for his glory, we were never meant to die. We were never meant to witness or experience the horror and indignity of death. It is an enemy—the result of our rebellion. And its power will be undone when Jesus comes again.

That being said, sometimes it can feel like a relief, like crossing the finish line of a long race run on rugged terrain. Foundational to the Christian hope and fundamental to our ability to endure hardship of any kind is knowing that it will not last forever, and that it will give way to glory. These days marred by sin and filled with its effects will come to an end when Jesus returns. Sin will cease. Evil will end. Death will be undone, and all of the wrong things will be made right. But until then, even while its sting remains, death is the doorway through which we enter the rest of God when our days of patient endurance come to their appointed end.

DEALING WITH MY CHILDHOOD

I wish I could say that when my mom died, my dad and I came together in our grief and sought the Lord for his comfort and healing. But that is not what happened at all. I loved my dad, but I was angry with him, and I resented his sorrow. In his weakness and sin, he had been so unkind to my mom—hateful even—and it felt unfair that he should miss her. I didn't know how to reconcile my own hurt and anger toward him with the example of compassion I saw in Jesus. I think I expected that because I loved the Lord, I should have been able to walk through difficulty and loss without struggling. And because I couldn't do that, I didn't know how to engage with my dad, and I wanted to pull away.

At the same time, I felt a strong and largely misplaced sense of responsibility for my dad. I worried about him constantly. I wanted to make sure he was OK and had every opportunity to know the love of God. But he was not always easy to care for, and I was not always patient and kind. I felt conflicted and guilty, powerless and responsible; I was a heroine and victim all in the same breath. My heart grew increasingly indignant and self-righteous.

After college, I returned to the Dallas area and began attending The Village Church. I started serving with children and was soon given the opportunity to come on staff. I loved teaching children about God's nature and character. Thinking of how to teach his word in a way that was accessible to them without compromising the truth of the text was the hardest and most fun thing I had done in ministry. I grew in love for God and his people in profound ways. And as I did, it became apparent that I needed help in facing my past and healing from it. Even though I was continuing to grow as a Christian and was experiencing the joy of fruitful ministry, there were things in my heart that were not right. I harbored unforgiveness, wrestled with unresolved loss, and struggled to process the effects of my turbulent childhood.

At that time, a ministry was developing at our church to help people consider both their past and present struggles in light of the gospel, and walk toward freedom by confessing those struggles, repenting of sin where needed, pursuing reconciliation with others, and living with a foundation of truth set firmly in place. It was called Steps. Walking through it, along with a season of counseling and the patient wisdom and presence of dear friends, changed my life.

As a child, the consistent refrain of my shame and fear was the vow that no one could ever know how broken and sad our family was. Having a safe space to tell the truth about those hard things opened the door for me to receive God's grace in the deepest and darkest places of my heart. I was able to extend forgiveness to others, put fear to death, and experience freedom from the anger and resentment that I thought kept me safe but really kept me bound.

In that same season, a passage and picture from the book of Jeremiah began to shape the vision of our ministry to children.

Thus says the LORD:
"Cursed is the man who trusts in man
and makes flesh his strength,
whose heart turns away from the LORD.
He is like a shrub in the desert,
and shall not see any good come.
He shall dwell in the parched places of the wilderness,
in an uninhabited salt land.

"Blessed is the man who trusts in the LORD,
whose trust is the LORD.
He is like a tree planted by water,
that sends out its roots by the stream,
and does not fear when heat comes,
for its leaves remain green,
and is not anxious in a year of drought,
for it does not cease to bear fruit."
(Jeremiah 17 v 5-8)

These verses show us what it looks like to know the Lord, to trust him deeply, and to bear fruit as we endure adversity, scarcity, and affliction. The tree described in this passage is flourishing, not because the climate is ideal but because it is connected to the source of life. The tree is planted by the stream because it is dependent upon the waters to sustain it in every season. Heat—the presence of painful and harmful circumstances—will come: adversity, affliction, and uncertainty. But the tree is not afraid. Drought—the absence of what is needed for life and flourishing—will come: seasons of scarcity, loneliness, and loss. But the tree is not anxious. It may be in pain, but it is not in danger. The water's flow is strong, protecting it and providing all that's needed for green leaves and good fruit. God calls us to trust him. It is in his will and by his power that we bear fruit, regardless of circumstance.

Suffering is an assumed reality in the Scriptures. The world is broken because of our sin, which means no one escapes hardship on this side of heaven. And we have an enemy who hates us and is actively seeking to devour us and destroy our faith. The Bible tells the stories of men and women who suffered greatly as a result of their own sin (for example, Moses in Exodus 2 v 11-15), the sin of others (Tamar in 2 Samuel 13 v 1-20) or the schemes of the enemy (the demon-possessed man in Luke 8 v 26-38), or simply because they are living in a broken world (the woman with the issue of blood, and Jairus' family, in Mark 5 v 21-43). Jesus told his followers to expect trouble in this life (John 16 v 33). Even the beautiful promise of Romans 8 v 28, that "for those who love God all things work together for good," presumes that all things—including very bad and hard things—happen to Christians.

Knowing and trusting the truth of God's character does not protect us from suffering, but it does protect us in the midst of it. When we are united to Christ by the Spirit, we are connected forever in relationship with the Father, the source of life. Placing our confidence and hope in him in-stead of in ourselves, other people or our circumstances pro-vides what we need in order to flourish, even in pain.

By grace, the Lord had planted me by the water and caused the roots of my heart to be sent out by the stream, the knowledge of him as a Father who is perfectly wise, gen-erous, loving, and good. Coming to know God as a heavenly Father of whom these things are true changed the way I saw my earthly father. Our relationship and his circumstances remained difficult, but as I started to heal, I was able to move through the world in a more loving way, particularly toward him. By no means did I walk it perfectly. I strug-gled with how to extend compassion while also maintaining boundaries. I responded in frustration, indignation, pride, and self-protection on many occasions. But instead of justi-fying my sin by pointing to his, my heart was being trained to sense the Spirit's conviction, repent, and ask God for help and wisdom. And though I did not realize it then, God was kindly preparing my heart for a season when sacrifice for my dad's sake would not be optional for me

HE DIED ON A TUESDAY

In the years that followed, my dad's health began to fail. I remember sitting with him when we saw the X-ray showing a mass in his chest. He had smoked for more decades than I had been alive, so it was pretty easy to understand what we were looking at. Life had been hard for him, and he had moved through it in a hard way. He had demonstrated in-credible endurance, but he was tired, and the prospect of his life coming to an end felt to him more like a relief, I think, than something to be resisted.

I was getting ready to face my greatest fear: the death of not just one but both of my parents. But unlike the little girl making contingency plans on the porch and trying to carry the weight of the world on her small shoulders, I knew that I was loved by God and that I was not alone. I didn't have to figure out how to provide for myself or anyone else. I knew his promises—to always and only do good to his children; to provide for, protect, and be with them—and I trusted him to be faithful. The One who was stronger than sin and death had heard my prayers with an attentive ear and had given me roots deep enough to endure the heat and drought ahead.

My dad died on a Tuesday, close to noon. He seemed peaceful as his breathing slowed and then stopped. I remem-ber the horrible moment days before when I realized that in order for his pain to be managed, he would have to stay asleep, which meant I would never be able to communicate with him again. Despite his failings and the difficulties of our relationship, I loved my dad. He was so much more than the hard and hurting man who had often felt like a storm looming on the horizon. He had a brilliant mind with a tireless work ethic. He was articulate and charming, and he knew his way around a grill. And he loved me. A lot. I knew that.

God's mercy and provision were more tangible in the days surrounding my dad's death than I had experienced before or have experienced since. He provided miraculously at every turn, largely through his people. From the first panicked phone call from my dad, telling me he could not move, to the moment of his last breath, I was never alone. At each point where a difficult decision needed to be made, from signing a DNR to options for hospice care to planning his memorial service, God made the right choice obvious or someone who loved me just took care of it. I was surrounded and carried by the church. They flooded into my most vulnerable moments with light, love, prayer, and most importantly, presence. I felt small and weak— like dust (Psalm 103 v 14). But for the first time, those feelings did not bring shame or fear. I was little but loved, small but safe. I knew the nearness of God, certainly by the Spirit living in me but also in the overwhelming presence of the Spirit living in other believers who loved and served me during this time.

God had indeed given me a family, and he was teaching me to live and walk in that reality.

HE MEETS US IN OUR MESS

In the weeks following my dad's passing, I joined a group of others in our church walking through grief. Together, we wept and shared about those we had lost. God ministered to me through their stories and the honesty of their struggle. I learned that grief wasn't something to "do," a task to be completed with perfection. Instead, I realized that grief doesn't actually end; it simply changes with time. That was liberating. There was no hurry, no timetable on how long it was acceptable to be sad and miss my dad, or my mom for that matter.

In the years since his death, I have continued to draw comfort from that lesson. The grief I experience for both of my parents has changed with time. The days I expect to be hard—the anniversaries of their passing, holidays where certain traditions had been formed, my birthday—are hard sometimes. But sometimes they're not. And that's OK. Then there are times when I'm blindsided by a memory and flooded with unexpected sadness. And that's OK, too.

I miss my parents, and I miss having parents. Even though I am a part of the church family and surrounded by brothers and sisters who love me, I still feel the sting, shame (misplaced as it may be), and vulnerability of not having a physical family to belong to. It's tempting to feel lost and alone in the world.

But God knows that. He knows the days he's given me and what has filled them. And in all of them, whether pleasant or painful, his intentions toward me have only ever been kind. He is faithfully working all things together for his glory and my good.

I know this to be true by looking at Jesus. God the Son entered the frailty of the human condition. He walked through the brokenness of this world and drew near to the lowly, broken, and vulnerable. When we look at Jesus, we see what God is like. When we see him restore a widow's son, we see what God is like (Luke 7 v 11-17). When we see him weep with Mary and Martha, even though he knew Lazarus was going to live, we see what God is like (John 11 v 17-35). When we see him quietly heal and then publicly bless that bleeding woman who had been afflicted and ashamed for over a decade, we see what God is like (Mark 5 v 25-34). Over and over, we see Jesus move toward the wounded and enter the most tender, shameful spaces with compassion and power. And in that, we see what God is like. He moves toward us in our mess and meets us there with love.

Indeed, Jesus has taken up our griefs and carried our sorrows (Isaiah 53 v 4). And for Jesus to carry our sorrows means that he has touched them. He is acquainted with all that has caused us pain, sadness, fear, and shame. In the same way that he extended his hand to the leper and said in word and deed, "I am willing; be cleansed" (Matthew 8 v 3), he puts his hands on our hurt and administers not only compassion but also the power to heal, redeem, and restore.

Jesus was himself a man of sorrows, acquainted with loneliness and loss. He knew anguish of soul, and was despised and rejected, accused and betrayed (Isaiah 53 v 1-3; Mark 14 v 32-72). He cried out to the Father for mercy in his time of need (Luke 22 v 41-44). Jesus suffered, greatly. And more than any other testimony, Jesus' example in suffering shows us how to endure hardship with hope and trust God's redemptive purposes (1 Peter 2 v 21-25).

Jesus' suffering accomplished our salvation, and our suffering is also accomplishing something beautiful. In and through it, God is refining our faith (Romans 5 v 1-5), glorifying his name (John 9 v 1-7), conforming us more to the image of his Son, and working all things together according to the wisdom of his will (Romans 8 v 28-29; Isaiah 46 v 8-11).

We will all suffer on this side of heaven. Even when our roots go deep, heat and drought will come. Paul assured the young believers of Lystra, Iconium, and Antioch that "we must go through many hardships to enter the kingdom of God" (Acts 14 v 22, NIV). That is true for us as well. But we do not need to be afraid. Like Jesus, we can entrust ourselves fully to the Father, trusting that we are safe and loved regardless of what seasons of scarcity or adversity he calls us to endure. He has given us his peace, the power of his Spirit, the family of his people, and the grace to count even the greatest sorrow as pure joy, knowing he is with us to the end and that, at the end, we shall be with him.

May 18, 2010

So today I had to do the MRI with perfusion, which just means that they push a lot of the contrast through you and then watch how it goes in and out of your brain and kind of tracks in the blood. Basically, where there's cancerous activity, there's a high amount of blood feeding the cancerous cells, and so they were looking around that cloud that I mentioned to see if there was a lot of blood flow around that. If there is a lot it shows up in the scan that they print out for me in red and yellow. If there was a lot of blood flow around that cloud that was going to be very bad news, and if there was no blood flow around then that was really good news.

So we did the scan this morning, and had lunch with some dear friends, and then we headed in to see the doctor. There are four elevators there, and right there a guy came up to me and just thanked me for these updates. He had actually just come down from the same doctor I was going up to see, and he had received really bad news. So I got a chance to hug him and pray with him, and then he prayed with me.

And then we headed upstairs—and the cloud had continued to shrink significantly, and there was no blood flow around the cloud, which basically means that that little bit of discoloration in the MRI is swelling or scar tissue from radiation. So they're not guessing that anymore—now they're pretty convinced of that. And so we will just continue to watch it.

I start another round of chemo this Sunday night, and so I will preach and then go home and start a round of chemo and will be on chemo this week, and then we have another MRI scheduled in July, so that'll be the next time we do an MRI.

So that was the news we found out today. It's very good news. All the doctors involved were very pleased by the results; we're very pleased by the results. There's this part of me that wishes there was this moment where they could just say, "It's a miracle" or "There's no explanation for this," but because of the type of cancer, it could very well be going on at the cellular level, even though without blood flow it can't grow. So they're never going say, "You're cured. This is miraculous." They're just going to be hopeful and continue to watch it.

We're going into this next round of chemo—the doctor was wanting (because the last one beat me up so bad) to take me off that amount, but she just looked at the chart again, and they can't do that. They've got to keep it up—they feel they are way ahead of this thing, and so they're just trying to crush every bit of it out.

9. MORE BROKEN AND MUCH BRIGHTER

Joy in the Sorrow of Life-Threatening Disease

Jonathan Woodlief

The movements here are slower, mechanical, and calculated. Deep breaths. It is almost as if the people here have danced on the preciousness of the precipice of life and are now realizing the sacredness of the ground they walk on.

I was dropped into an environment like this for the first time about 22 years ago, and decades later the whole scene is now commonplace, even comfortable, for me. Colors of white, gray, and black. A stale smell—the aroma you would get if you combined the smells of latex, plastic, and blood. Waiting and "what ifs" provide the central soundtrack. There's enough silence to hear a needle drop, and at times there are too many tears for one space. You spend so long with them that you become a new family, forged by pain and scars.

Suffering is the common denominator of all humanity in this world, isn't it? All of us are marked by scars of some sort, though not all are ones you can see. Waiting rooms and hospitals and gravesites don't play favorites. Rich and poor.

Old and young. Every ethnicity and every generation. All under the same curse of a broken and bruised world where things don't work the way they were supposed to. Suffering is a part of every human experience.

We all have a preferred future. Hopes of what life will look like years from now. A story that we've written about how things could and should be for our lives. A story noticeably free of waiting, tears and scars.

Well, for me, all that came crashing down when I was 13 and was plunged into a world of waiting and "what-ifs."

SOMETHING CALLED LUPUS

It began with flu-like symptoms. I draped over our couch like an antique blanket. I lay there for hours when I would normally be up and about, watching sports and playing outside. My entire body felt as if it was under a type of malaise. Hot and cold. Achy joints. And then a strange rash covered my nose and face in the shape of a butterfly. Doctor after doctor. And then emergency room after emergency room. And no diagnosis for months.

Eventually, a diagnosis came. I remember my dad saying, "Well, at least it's not cancer." We were all just thankful for some type of direction and answer. I wrote in my journal, "I've been diagnosed with something called lupus."

Something called lupus.

Lupus is most common in African-American women of childbearing age. So, when I received this diagnosis as a white youth at 13, it was pretty shocking to my family. Lupus is an autoimmune disease, which generally means that your white blood cells become confused, so instead of fighting off illness and disease, they begin to attack your own body. In the most severe cases, lupus attacks internal organs, and it is usually fatal in adolescent males. Like me.

The lupus was already attacking my kidneys.

The condition would only be compounded from there. While my family was hopeful that this would quickly become a thing of the past, it intensified as the months and even years began to pass. The doctors put me on chemo treatment in order to curb the aggressive form of the disease that was beginning to damage my kidneys. The treatment made a difference to how much I threw up, but not to my blood counts. It seemed as if there wasn't much hope.

What do you do in these moments? These are the times of wrestling and questioning. The weeping. The waiting and worrying. The I'm-not-sure-I-can-make-it moments. Your mind races days, weeks, months, and years into the future. Your anxieties roar with "what-ifs." There was something in me that tried to discount circumstances, thinking it would all be over soon and I would get well. There was part of me that wondered if I'd done something wrong. But in the midst of it all, God was gracious to give me a view of him big enough to absorb the weight of the coming years, or the lack of them.

One of my favorite things about God is that he is involved in the details of our lives. He doesn't make mistakes. He isn't surprised when bad things happen. And the Scriptures paint the picture of a God who isn't just in control over the big things in life like oceans, tornadoes, and thunder. He's intimately involved with the intricacies of his creation as well. He isn't just sovereign over lightning bolts; he is sovereign over lightning bugs. He doesn't just number stars; Matthew 10 v 30 tells us he numbers the hairs on our head (easier for some than others).

One narrative in Scripture that really began to grab hold of my attention during this dark season was the life of Joseph. One of the most beautiful things about the story is that it shows that nothing can stop God's plan—that God is orchestrating every single detail for his good purposes. In the story, which took place around 1700-1600 BC, Joseph is pretty arrogant and, despite being one of the youngest of the brothers, assures his siblings that one day they'll bow to him (a fairly typical younger sibling, in some ways). Not only that, but he's his dad's favorite. Joseph's brothers, consumed by envy and anger, plot to kill Joseph and then end up selling him to slave traders who sell him in Egypt. Through the next years of his life, Joseph is falsely accused, forgotten in prison, lied about, used, and threatened—but one of the overarching truths is that neither mistakes nor the sins of others nor the mishaps of Joseph can stop the sovereign plan of God. In Genesis 45, as Joseph (now the Egyptian Pharaoh's right-hand man) is reunited with his brothers, he emphasizes three specific times to them that "it was not you who sent me here, but God" (v 8, see also v 5 and 7). Genesis 50 v 20 is the more well-known restatement of this truth: "As for you, you meant evil against me, but God meant it for good, to bring it about that many people should be kept alive, as they are today."

Our God isn't the author of evil, but he is stronger than evil, and so he gets to use evil for his purposes, and not the other way around. Our King always acts with purpose—and not one plan of his can be thwarted, for his counsel "stands forever" (Psalm 33 v 11).

And so we held on to the idea that our suffering wasn't without purpose: that God wasn't surprised and he still was working a good plan. This gave us hope. And we were going to cling to hope, even if just by a few threads, in the months to come.

GRACE BEATS KARMA

Around the age of 17, the doctors became uncertain that continuing chemotherapy would do the trick. The treatments had been pummeling my body for two years straight. My weekly rhythm had been to miss Fridays and Mondays of school, and throw up from the toxicity of the treatments over the weekends. I didn't lose my hair during this time, but everything else seemed to be slipping from my grip. I hadn't grown for three years, since before I was diagnosed. Some combination of all the medicines compounded by the disease had stunted my growth. I also had a lot in common with any family friends who were 80 and older. Medicare. Bone issues (I had osteoporosis at the time, again from the medications). Too many prescriptions to keep count of. I used to joke with my friends that I did more drugs and missed more school than all of them combined. And on top of it all, I had stopped playing basketball. In many ways the saddest thing, for me and those who knew me, wasn't just that I couldn't bounce a ball but that I didn't want to. Basketball had been a sign of life and hope for me, and when the ball stopped bouncing, it was almost as if I didn't see a future anymore.

We had been running to every possible solution, and nothing seemed to work. We had prayed and asked for healing. I'd been treated by some of the best doctors and lupus specialists we could find. We ate every green plant known to man. Vegetable and fruit diets. Fasts. Enemas. Probiotics. Chiropractors. Metal toxin treatments. Magnets. Any health fad that you have heard of—we were most likely trying it around this time, desperate for help.

And one of the things I learned is how easy it is for those good things to become ultimate things—idols—to us. Our culture tends to tell people that healthy lifestyles will save, cure, and heal all. And then when people don't get well, we act as if they got it wrong. Maybe they didn't do the diet right. Maybe they didn't take the alternative medicines enough. Maybe they did something else wrong.

This karma-like thinking is seriously damaging, and it has no place among the people of God.

"Karma says, *You sin, you pay.* Grace says, *You sin, God pays.* The Scriptures teach that grace wins."

#JOYINTHESORROW

It's too simplistic: just like Job's friends, who thought everything he was suffering was a direct result of personal sin (Job 4 – 5; 8).

It's too narrow, like the disciples who figured the man born blind was like that because of either his own mistakes or those of his parents (John 9 v 1-3).

It's too limiting a view of sickness and suffering, just like the view of the people in Jesus' time who didn't realize that sometimes bad things—like a tower in Siloam falling and crushing 18 people—do happen, and it's not because those people did the wrong things while others did the right ones (Luke 13 v 4-5).

The Scriptures teach grace, not karma. Karma says, *You sin, you pay.* Grace says, *You sin, God pays.* So if we understand the Scriptures, we realize that if karma ruled, we'd experience far worse than we do. And the Scriptures teach us that since grace wins, in Christ we can and one day will enjoy far better than we ever should. But for now, we live in a broken world where things aren't as they should be. Bad things happen, and it stinks. And sometimes bad times come to people who have been doing things right, and vice versa.

But for the Christian, these bad things aren't punishments from God. They aren't paybacks for our mistakes. Jesus already took all of those mistakes on the cross. He paid it all: "For our sake [God] made him to be sin who knew no sin, so that in him we might become the righteousness of God" (2 Corinthians 5 v 21). Nothing else has to be paid back because his grace covers all.

And so as Christians, we confidently hope for the day when all things will be made right. The renewal and restoration of all things in Jesus is our hope. We had to remind ourselves that our ultimate hope wasn't in a treatment plan, lab results, a doctor's prognosis, or a different doctor's alternative plan.

God is good, and in what is often called his "common grace" he gives good gifts like good food, doctors, oils, and treatments. These are hope-giving, but they aren't our ultimate Hope. They cannot bear that burden. They cannot wipe away suffering for all time. Only Jesus can do that.

ENTER KIDNEY, ENTER GIRL

Amid deflated basketballs and seemingly no cures from the medical world, our hopes for my life dwindled. My kidneys failed, and the doctors told my parents I'd need to go on dialysis. It started with six months on peritoneal dialysis, where the doctors attached a tube in my stomach that would connect me to a machine to do the job that my kidneys normally would, for about ten hours each night. However, after about six months, I got a massive infection and was hospitalized. Peritonitis, pancreatitis, a feeding tube and six weeks in the hospital left our entire family in a low state. I started a different type of dialysis, where I had a port in my chest and would go for the treatment three times a week. I wasn't yet 18.

The Lord has a way of bringing people into your life and showing his providence in your life, which helps you keep going. I heard someone once say that the gospel creates family where there isn't family. For some, and maybe for you as you read, the church has left a bad taste in the mouth— but we had the privilege of experiencing the exact opposite: of seeing church be the community that God intends and commands it to be.

The Lord brought a doctor into our life who became a father figure to me: Dr. James Tumlin. He treated me like a person and not just a patient: as someone made in the image of God and not just a diagnosis. Dr. T. would sit down with my two sisters and mom, and counsel and encourage them after meeting with me. He would invite me to a ball game, or invite our family over for dinner. He would encourage us that all hope was not lost and that God was still working.

Pastors at church mowed our lawn. Families from church brought us meals. They signed up to take shifts in driving me to dialysis or picking me up. People gave money so we could walk through the times when we were drowning financially in hospital bills and inordinately expensive treatments. They wrote cards. Proverbs talks about a fitting word for a season (Proverbs 25 v 11), and sometimes it felt like a word came just when we were about to give up all hope. The school where my mom worked gave us money to get alternative treatment. We would happen upon envelopes containing cash that simply pointed us to the Lord as being the great Provider. With each word and each loving action, the Lord was reminding us that he was for us and with us. Encouragement at its root carries the idea of imparting or breathing courage into someone, and the family of God helped us lift our heads when we didn't know what else to do. It was a glimpse of hope in a dark place. Psalm 27 v 13-14 says:

> I would have despaired unless I had believed I would
> see the goodness of the LORD
> in the land of the living.
> Wait for the LORD;
> be strong and let your heart take courage;
> yes, wait for the LORD. (NASB)

During my senior year, my family started getting tested to give me a kidney. My dad wasn't able to give me his kidney because of some blood-pressure issues, but my mom ended up being a match. So, four days after I graduated high school, my mom gave me her kidney, and for the first time in five years I started regaining health. My bones started to normalize. I came off dialysis. My medicines were tapered off, and I even started to grow again as the kidney began to kick in and work. After six years of battling, I had a long reprieve from kidney problems and hospital stays.

About nine years after my kidney transplant, I met a girl. Caitlin Conneally walked into a room and stole the show. We were friends at first, and then (after she rejected me a few times) we began to date.

I didn't want to tell Cait about my illness. To me, it was the worst of me—something that would scare her away. Because of years of chemo, there was a high chance that I couldn't have children. Because of years of immunosuppressive drugs, I was at a heightened risk of things like cancer, diabetes, and glaucoma. There was even a chance that lupus could come back again. I had scars all over my body—scars from dialysis tubes in my stomach and neck, scars from kidney transplants—and I carried emotional scars of that time that I didn't even know were there. To be honest, I sort of felt like damaged goods because of these things.

When I got around to telling my story, Caitlin shocked me by saying she wasn't surprised. She told me that she had seen in me a compassion for people that made her feel that God had brought me through something. At the time, we left it at that. But the conversation was pushed up sooner than we would have liked.

There is one line of thinking in the world that is surprised by any type of suffering, and I for sure would have landed in that camp at one point. There is another strand of faulty thinking that believes our suffering is measured in cups or ounces or whatever your serving size, but that at some point God has doled out a sufficient amount upon us, and we are through. It's as if we forget we are still living in the tension of "already but not yet"—that though we are

God's forgiven people, his children, things aren't as they are supposed to be in this world. We are not home with him yet. And so we are not through with walking through sorrows yet.

WHY *NOT* ME?

About a year into my relationship with Caitlin, my ankles started swelling. This brought the flashbacks of kidney disease. After a few blood tests at Dallas Transplant Institute and weeks of waiting, the diagnosis came: kidney disease. Caitlin and I were wanting to move toward marriage. Suddenly our plans were on shaky ground.

From there, the disease just seemed to steamroll from one level of difficulty to another. Though doctors had told me lupus only comes back in 2% of transplanted kidneys, it was indeed systemic lupus attacking this kidney again. I started back on chemotherapy. The doctor's visits, biopsies and dialysis conversations began all over again. I didn't know what to do.

As all this was going on, our pastor, Matt Chandler, was battling brain cancer and being treated with chemotherapy. One of the most meaningful things we heard him say is that our common response to suffering is "Why me?" And we were feeling this especially. How could it happen again? At this time? To me, and now to Caitlin? However, Chandler would point out that for the person who reads the Bible, their question should move to "Why *not* me?"

If you're willing to see, the Bible is full of those who suffered, and yet whom God used. Moses led complaining Israelites wandering around the desert for 40 years. Joseph was sold into slavery, betrayed, put in prison and forgotten, and didn't see God's redemption for 20 years. Hannah was barren. Ruth's husband died. Bathsheba was taken advantage of by the king. Job lost everything he held dear in one day. John the Baptist was beheaded. Timothy had stomach issues. The apostle Paul had a thorn in the flesh and experienced shipwrecks, beatings, and just the weariness of leading the church. The disciple John was exiled to the island of Patmos. Mary Magdalene was treated by many like the scum of the earth. James tells us we will have "various trials" (James 1 v 2). Peter tells us to "not be surprised at the fiery trial" (1 Peter 4 v 12). Jesus himself says, "If they persecuted me, they will also persecute you" (John 15 v 20). Western culture says *Run from suffering* and some cultures say *Run to it*, but the Scriptures encourage us to walk with God in the midst of it. This was one of the central balms for my soul: expect suffering. We all know that this world isn't the way it's supposed to be. But even more as Christians, we expect hardship as we follow a Savior who carried a cross.

That may not sound like a balm to the soul! But it is, because it's only when we stand in that place that we can then enjoy the truth that Jesus is with us and for us in our suffering, and leading us through it. This was a truth that made our hearts sing all the way through. When I was first diagnosed with lupus, my mom was memorizing Psalm 34 in the few weeks before it all broke loose. To this day, there is a verse plastered with tape that hangs in the shower at my mom's house—Psalm 34 v 18: "The LORD is near to the brokenhearted and saves the crushed in spirit."

Even still, it was hard. Very hard. Christ's presence and Christ's hope don't make it easy. Sometimes we felt like we couldn't take one more step. It was as if someone had knocked the breath out of our lungs and the breath out of our souls simultaneously. Darkness, even despair, covered us, and we were paralyzed with fear and "what ifs." I remember that one day, when Caitlin and I were in the midst of prayer gatherings for healing and believing that God was able to change the circumstances, we received another lab

"Western culture says *Run from suffering* and some cultures say *Run to it,* but the Scriptures encourage us to walk with God in the midst of it."

#JOYINTHESORROW

result showing continued deteriorated kidney function. We sat in the parking lot and wept.

Cait's mom was in town that day, and we all went back to my apartment. I picked up a book about Jesus' sufferings, and we just began to read. And in a moment only those who have walked it can describe, I just felt the peace of Jesus. We read about how Jesus is a sympathetic Savior.

Hebrews 4 v 15-16 tells us:

> For we do not have a high priest who is unable to sympathize with our weaknesses, but one who in every respect has been tempted as we are, yet without sin. Let us then with confidence draw near to the throne of grace, that we may receive mercy and find grace to help in time of need.

Days of darkness and difficulty? Jesus knows. Temptation? Jesus knows. The sting and pain of death and losing a friend? He knows. Unbearable pain? Jesus knows it. Denial, betrayal and abandonment? Jesus has felt it. Anguish beyond our ability to cope? Jesus has experienced it. In the words of the author Beth Moore, "He knows it's scary to be us." These truths would help bear the weight of some of the news we were about to receive.

"HE HIDES A SMILING FACE"

A group of our friends pooled money together and helped us get to Atlanta, Georgia, to visit with the doctor who had performed my first transplant. We continued to hold out hope for healing—either that God would miraculously heal my kidney or that he would provide another kidney match. This meeting was to do two things: first, to diagnose the health of my kidney; second, to see how many antibodies my body had. Essentially, antibodies are created through organ transplants, blood transfusions and pregnancy. I had experienced the first two (and not, obviously, the third!), making for a more difficult match, but we were hopeful my antibodies were not too high.

When the results came back, we learned that my kidney was limping along at about 7% of normal function and that I already should have been on dialysis. We also learned that my antibodies were extremely high: 99%. This was a soul-punching type of news. I needed a new kidney. The doctors said I would probably be on dialysis for about 10 to 15 years waiting for a match because our probability of finding a match to my tissues, antibodies and all, was in the one-out-of-millions chance range.

The meeting sent me into a spiral of depression. I was unable to journal or write. Unable to articulate my thoughts well. We felt like someone had put our brains on a roller-coaster and left our stomachs in the air. I was confused. Sick. Uncertain. I was 29, and Cait and I were hoping to get married the coming fall. This was not the life I'd planned for myself, or wanted for her.

Pastor Matt was still on and off chemo and getting brain scans, and I'll never forget what he said from the pulpit. "God is God. And statistics are statistics. Everything is subservient to him." It echoed the truths from the story of Joseph that I had clung to from a young age. Statistics aren't God. They are helpful, but they don't trump the plans of God. No plan of his can be dismantled or thwarted. All things are from his hands, and his hands are good hands. His hands are pure and providential, guiding every step of our lives. And this is true even when we can't see it or feel it. He is always at work. Even in weeping times, in waiting times, in the worst of times. His ways are mysterious. As William Cowper wrote:

God moves in a mysterious way
His wonders to perform;
He plants his footsteps in the sea
And rides upon the storm ...

Ye fearful saints, fresh courage take;
The clouds ye so much dread
Are big with mercy and shall break
In blessings on your head.

Judge not the Lord by feeble sense,
But trust him for his grace;
Behind a frowning providence
He hides a smiling face.

THE MEDICAL LIGHTNING STRIKE

And so we waited. And our waiting was difficult. Waiting in faith is not just about smiling lots and telling everyone happily that you're trusting God. In the psalms, it often looks like crying out, "How long, O LORD?" (Try reading Psalms 13, 35, and 90.) Waiting is hard, and often it feels like just clinging on.

Caitlin and I got married that October. I still desperately needed a kidney transplant. In November, I was put on the transplant list, and then over the next few months friends and family started coming out of the woodwork to get tested. Two of our close friends in Dallas and then two close friends in New Hampshire all got tested. Caitlin joined in that batch; she wanted to get tested as well.

So the next January, a day was set when everyone was tested. And Caitlin and I began getting calls that day. Richard is not a match. Erin is not a match. Craig and Karissa are not matches. And then finally, a nurse called Caitlin and said, "No one is a match." And then—after the most dramatic pause known to man—she continued, "... except you."

How in the world? How could this be?

Caitlin is the match.

My wife? When my doctors heard, they said it was a "medical lightning strike," whatever that means. Some said it was at least a 1 in 10 million chance that it could happen. We just called it a miracle. We were stunned. In tears. Still scared. But trusting in our God, we started moving forward to a kidney transplant.

When our story went out on the news, there were all sorts of reactions, but they basically fell into two categories. There were overly sentimental ones where people said things like, "They are the perfect match!" "A match made in heaven!" "Must be nice to have everything go perfectly for you!" And then others were deeply cynical. "They will be divorced in five years." "I reckon they are siblings. Creepy." "I bet he has an affair, and it ends awful."

But the truth is that those next six months toward the transplant fitted neither of those categories. And the seven years or so since our kidney transplant proved to be neither of those pictures, either. The good news of the gospel fights both a naive optimism and a disillusioned pessimism, because it simultaneously says that things are more broken and sad than we realize, but also brighter and more hopeful than we might imagine.

Caitlin gave me her kidney six months later, on June 18th. And it started working. It's still working, seven years later. We have two children. We hope for more, but right now we have two little miracle babies, showing the kindness of God and the work of God in the worst times.

But I can tell you that this isn't our "happily ever after." We left that hospital room that summer and were plastered across ABC News, Yahoo, and the Huffington Post as a perfect story. But we also left that room bearing scars. Matching physical scars from the surgery. Emotional scars that stung with pain every time a blood test would look poor, or each time I was hospitalized because of potential kidney rejection or side effects from medicines. And there are other scars that a community bears when they walk through both the valleys and the mountaintops together.

The thing about the scars on my body is that I used to hate them. I used to be embarrassed of them. But now I know they tell a bigger story of a restoring and always-at-work God, who reigns amid the mess. Now I know they tell a story of reality—that we must expect brokenness in this life and in our bodies. We are to expect tears, even as we experience the presence of our good God in the midst of those times.

But the scars remind me of another thing—hope. The longing in all of us for the scars and sadness to be made right again, and the knowledge that they will be.

Revelation 21, the penultimate chapter of Scripture, points us to a certain future day:

> *Then I saw a new heaven and a new earth, for the first heaven and the first earth had passed away, and the sea was no more. And I saw the holy city, new Jerusalem, coming down out of heaven from God, prepared as a bride adorned for her husband. And I heard a loud voice from the throne saying, "Behold, the dwelling place of God is with man. He will dwell with them, and they will be his people, and God himself will be with them as their God. He will wipe away every tear from their eyes, and death shall be no more, neither shall there be mourning, nor crying, nor pain anymore, for the former things have passed away."*

And he who was seated on the throne said, "Behold, I am making all things new." Also he said, "Write this down, for these words are trustworthy and true."

(v 1-5)

Jesus' cross was temporary, and our burdens will be too. And when Jesus rose from his tomb, he rose physically, in a body that still bore the scars of his sufferings. His scars remind us that he knows what it's like and that he cared enough to do something about it.

Edward Shillito, in his poem "Jesus of the Scars," says it like this:

But to our wounds only God's wounds can speak,
And not a god has wounds, but Thou alone.

One day, there will be no more tears and no more pain. No more death. No more mourning. No more kidney issues. Everything made new, by those nail-scarred hands.

August 6, 2010

Sorry it's been so long since we posted an update. It's been five or six weeks and we're doing real well. My last scan was two weeks ago, and they were actually more pleased with it than they were with my last scan, which they were very pleased with! There was one little mark in the scan. It was what they call a leaking vessel. I was like, "Is that an aneurysm?"—but they don't seem to be worried about it, so neither am I.

The news that wasn't frustrating but was somewhat deflating is that they had originally said the chemo was gonna be 12 to 18 months, and—despite the fact that all my scans have been clean up until this point— they've officially called it 18 months now. So I have 12 rounds of chemo left. But the last round—the one we just completed last week—was probably the best round we had ever been through. There was only one day that was kind of nasty and then the rest of it was OK.

So thank you for your continued prayers. I continue to walk in and claim that I've been healed by God; the doctors continue to think that this thing's at a cellular level and it'll try to rear its head again. But one way or the other, he's good, and we're living like he's sovereign over all things and loves us deeply as his children. So again thank you so much for your prayers.

10. SOMEHOW, THIS IS ENOUGH

Joy in the Sorrow of Miscarriage
and Childlessness

Lore Ferguson Wilbert

Our first fight as a couple happened six weeks before the wedding. What's surprising is not that it took us so long but that neither of us even knew it was conflict until our pre-marital counselor smirked a sideways grin and said, "I'm interested to see how you work out this conflict." Nate and I are both soft-spoken and peace-loving people, so our disagreement contained about as much angst as some people bring to fights over what to have for dinner or which show to watch. The source of our conflict? We both desired children, but I wanted to be married a year before we started trying, and he wanted to wait until our wedding night.

In hindsight, what strikes me most about conflicts and fights over things of this nature is that we think the thing we're fighting over is within our full control. The timing of when to start having children, or stop having them, or the having of them at all, seemed to be as simple as deciding where to go for vacation or, well, what to eat for dinner. It seemed to be a given, something we assumed would happen, the timing within our control.

We decided to wait a year.

A SURPLUS OF SUFFERING

We moved to Colorado from Texas on the night of our wedding. My husband continued to work remotely for his job, and I came on staff at a rapidly growing church in a major city. We bought a rambling and quirky old farmhouse on a city corner, once the only house for acres when it was built in the 1890s. I sketched garden ideas, and we walked every night around our new neighborhood, dreaming of the future there together.

I don't remember what changed my mind, but two months after the wedding, we threw preventions out and prayed that God would open my womb. I was 34, Nate was 38, and we had begun thinking about the future, the far-ahead one where our child would be 20 and we'd be nearly 40 years their senior. It just made sense. A month later I was pregnant.

Everyone knows that suffering is part of life, but what no one warns you is that sometimes suffering comes in spades. Through the cloud of the first blow, when we're still reeling from its effects, we can't see the next one clearly, and that compounds things, making them seem worse than they are.

Two months after we moved I came home from work bearing sad news: the church where I was on staff was about to go through a reckoning process. We didn't know it then, but it would eclipse our entire lives for nearly a year. We had come from The Village Church in Texas, which had been family to us. We knew no church was perfect, but we didn't anticipate so much struggle right from the start.

That was my news. But Nate also had some. He sat across from me, in the farmhouse his paycheck paid for, and said,

"They're doing cutbacks and because I'm remote, I'm the first to go."

Two days later, I began to bleed, profusely and painfully. There was a strange optimism in me, though. I was 34, this was my first pregnancy, and we were stressed, so the risks were higher. These were the things I told myself, adding each of them together until they equaled miscarriage. One in four pregnancies ends in miscarriage, I knew the statistics, and I was just one of them. A fluke. I didn't weep at all. I felt beaten, but also resilient. Things were going to be OK.

Every day I came home from work that fall while my husband searched for a job. Every day I came home to the sound of a popular worship song, the chorus of which says only "You are good" on repeat. It became the anthem of our autumn. We were sure God's goodness would result in peace at church, a good job for Nate, and children for us eventually.

The thing about God's goodness—the thing we have spent the whole of our marriage learning—is that it doesn't cease even when all around us goodness feels lost. God's goodness isn't a gift he doles out. His goodness is his character. It's who he is. Because it's who he is, it's all he does. Everything he does is good because he is good.

By the first week of January, we were expecting a baby again, and beginning to dream of names and baby toes and fingers. I spent the same week with the rest of our church staff in critical meetings with church leaders, members, deacons, and more. The last day of the week, the whole membership gathered in the sanctuary to hear where the chaos of the last few months had led. I was exhausted. We all were. It seemed as though we'd been in nonstop meetings for weeks. I stood at the back of the sanctuary, listening as painful news was delivered to the congregation, and felt a sharp and shooting pain nearly buckling my knees, and a rush of blood again.

This one was faster, furious, and painful. I leaned against the wall of the bathroom stall downstairs, telling myself to relax, breathe, just breathe. When I could stand again, I left. I sobbed for hours in Nate's arms at home.

THE NEARNESS OF GOD

My ESV Bible translates Psalm 73 v 28 as "For me it is good to be near God," seemingly putting the onus on me to draw near to the Lord. But January's double blow of the church chaos and second miscarriage felt worse than September's triple, and finding the strength to draw near to God seemed impossible. We huddled together, prayed together, wept together, and tried to put ourselves in the way of God's goodness. But nothing felt good in those months. We put our house on the market, packed it up, and prepared to move across the country again, to Nate's new job on the east coast.

Our first conflict over when to have children seemed small and inconsequential. We were hemorrhaging money. It took five months to sell our house and we eventually lost close to $100k on it. After a year in the throes of a painful church crisis, we were burnt out and suspicious of certain church models and structures. We were alone in our new city. Nate's commute was three hours each day. I felt like a shell of the person I had been only a year before—that joyful, expectant, "about to be married and start her dream job" woman. I *was* a shell of that person.

I felt like a walking tomb, my only purpose to house death. My body felt like a betrayal of everything I felt sure of. I saw a doctor, and she ran some blood tests and said the miscarriages were probably due to stress and I should get counseling. But I felt swallowed in grief. I sleep-walked through the year in many ways, bearing the miscarriages as they came again and again, unsure of how to de-stress myself enough to the point where my body could carry a baby to term, or even past the first month. I ached with the brokenness we were experiencing in a world—in a body—not yet whole. I cried with Paul, "Who will rescue me from this body of death?" (Romans 7 v 24).

Somewhere in that year, the cloud parted. It didn't happen all at once or in some spectacular way. It was, in hindsight, the goodness of God breaking through what I could not part or parse on my own. Nate's Bible, an NASB, translates Psalm 73 v 28 like this: "The nearness of God is my good." Here, the onus is on God to be near me. He began to show me that he hadn't left at all and nothing I could do could put me more in his way if I tried. No matter how broken I felt, how much of a walking tomb I felt, or how far from God I felt, he was still drawing near to me. He was near me, and this reality was my only good.

THE GIFT IN THE LACK

I was single for 34 years and spent most of them desiring marriage. I knew a simple desire for a thing didn't guarantee the getting of it. God doesn't promise everyone marriage, despite the unhelpful churchy clichés that "God has a spouse for you." I had come to marriage knowing that it was an unmerited gift, that nothing I had done or not done had earned it for me, that it would not fix anything wrong with me, and that worshiping at its throne would only result in heartbreak and pain. At some point it occurred to me that all the same things were true of children, and, just as singleness had been a gift to me in its time, ordained by God for my good and his glory, childlessness could be too.

It began small inside me: this sense of seeing God's gift in our lack. It's an unpopular sentiment, even in the church. We rightly call children blessings because God calls them blessings, but could the absence of them also perhaps be a

"However God's
nearness comes—in
silence, in greatness,
in provision, in lack—
it is enough."

#JOYINTHESORROW

blessing? Could God still be good and therefore do good by withholding one blessing (children) and in its place giving another, stranger and unsought, blessing (childlessness)?

Could God be enough for me, for us, for our marriage, for our home, for my body, if we never saw what was never promised to us in God's word?

This subtle shift in my soul began to change everything. The nearness of children or the promise of them were not my good. The nearness of God was my only good, and I was learning that however his nearness comes—in silence, in greatness, in provision, in lack, in fullness, or in meagerness—it is enough.

There is a traditional song sung at the Jewish celebration of Passover. Its name is Dayenu, literally translated from Hebrew as "It would have been enough" or "It would have been sufficient" or "It would have sufficed." There are fifteen stanzas, each one building on the work of God on behalf of the people of God through the Old Testament:

"If he had only brought us out of Egypt, it would have been sufficient. If he had split the sea, it would have been enough. If he had given the Torah, it would have been sufficient."

On and on it goes, until the final verse: "If he had built the temple for us, it would have been enough." But because those who are reciting the stanzas miss the reality that the story of captivity, release, provision, and the creation of the temple is one grand illustration of the gospel, the song ends there for them.

Yet, we who are in Christ can add verse after verse after verse for all eternity, knowing true Dayenu through the life, death, and resurrection of Christ: if God had only done this one thing, it would have been sufficient. The book of Hebrews uses the phrase "once for all" in reference to Christ's sacrifice for us:

*He has no need, like those high priests, to offer
sacrifices daily, first for his own sins and then for
those of the people, since he did this once for all when
he offered up himself. (Hebrews 7 v 27)*

*He has appeared once for all at the end of the ages
to put away sin by the sacrifice of himself. And just
as it is appointed for man to die once, and after that
comes judgment, so Christ, having been offered once
to bear the sins of many, will appear a second time,
not to deal with sin but to save those who are eagerly
waiting for him. (Hebrews 9 v 26b-28)*

*We have been sanctified through the offering of the
body of Jesus Christ once for all. (Hebrews 10 v 10)*

One time and for all, his death was sufficient. And it is and
always will be sufficient. This portion we have in Christ,
with children or without them, is sufficient. Christ is
enough.

Psalm 73 continues: "Whom have I in heaven *but you?*
And there is *nothing* on earth that I desire besides *you*. My
flesh and my heart may fail, but God is the strength of my
heart and my *portion* forever" (v 25-26, emphasis mine).

This belief carried me. This song of Dayenu—the full
sufficiency of Christ for all our wants, needs, desires, and
every promise of God—quieted me. I finally felt at peace
with the lack, with not even asking God to do more than he
already had. He was sufficient. He was my portion. Nothing
on earth would satisfy like him. It was enough.

He quieted my body too. The miscarriages stopped for a
time, or if they came, they were so early they were mostly
undetectable. Perhaps it was a lessening of stress, or perhaps
just grace. We settled into a life of childlessness. We moved
cross-country again, back to Texas, where we'd first met in

the church foyer at The Village, back near our church family. We bought a house and invited a few young people to live with us. We determined to give our finances and time and energy to hospitality, to filling the corners of our home—if not with our own children, then with God's children.

OUT OF PLACE

One mid-June morning I was leaning over our vegetable garden, pulling small weeds. It was our first vegetable garden in Texas, and it needed a kind of tender, loving care that—being from the northeast originally, where you can throw seeds on a pile of dirt and they'll grow—I was unaccustomed to. As I leaned over, I felt a twinge in my abdomen unlike any I'd felt before. I didn't think I was pregnant, but I began spotting and thought, *Here we go again.*

I waited a week and nothing changed: the spotting continued, the twinges in my belly continued, but otherwise I felt great. *Maybe,* I thought, *I am pregnant, and this is what it's supposed to feel like. Maybe this is good.* I still thought it was too early to take a test, and I'd know sooner or later whether I was pregnant or not, so I continued on.

One evening, two weeks later, as we got ready for bed, I doubled over in pain. It was so intense that I couldn't breathe. I am not given to histrionics or exaggeration. I will do anything to avoid going to the doctor or hospital, and my pain tolerance is high. But after a few minutes of me protesting that I was fine, Nate told me we were leaving for the ER. We had no way of knowing it would be almost a week before I could come home.

They put me in a bed, ran an IV, put me on morphine, and drew blood. Somewhere in the fog of it all, the doctor came in and asked if I'd ever miscarried or had pregnancy complications. "Yes," we said: "Plenty of them."

"Did you know you are pregnant right now?" he asked.

I'd suspected that, I told him—I'd been spotting for two weeks and thought it might be implantation bleeding.

"It's worse," he said. "We can't be sure until we run more tests, but I suspect your pregnancy is…"

"Ectopic?" I interrupted him.

"Yes," he said, his eyes flickering down.

An ectopic pregnancy means, literally, an out of place pregnancy. For us, it appeared to be inside one of my fallopian tubes. It was unviable, and if left alone, the doctor said, I would rupture and would almost certainly die.

Is God sufficient in these moments? I felt the enemy laughing at me. *Who's your only good now?*

"We have to terminate or you could die," the doctor said. "Terminate" is not a word I ever thought I would use in the same thought as "baby." To me, these words are intrinsically at odds with one another. A baby is something you keep, I thought, even in my morphine-clouded and pain-addled mind. A baby is not something you surgically remove or induce a miscarriage for. I don't know what kind of strength came over me in this moment, but everyone else in the room seemed certain that this was the route we needed to go, and I knew I couldn't.

I COULD STILL ASK

We'd begun singing a song in our church a few weeks previously. The lyrics spoke of nature and science obeying God's words and revealing his nature. I would say them on repeat, singing it to myself in my hospital bed. In all these years, God had taught me about his sufficiency, but what I hadn't learned all the way through was that, like Jesus in the Garden of Gethsemane, I could also ask for what I wanted even if it wasn't promised. I could trust God's nearness, his goodness, his completeness, and still ask for more. I didn't have to, and needed not to, put my trust in getting the thing I wanted—but

God was nevertheless a good Father, and I could ask him for what I wanted. And I could ask knowing that, because he was good, I could trust that if he withheld what I desired, that too was for my good. He is a Father who knows how to give good gifts—supremely, himself (Luke 11 v 13).

Knowing all things are in submission to the sound of God's voice, and that anything can move, evolve, or shift into what God tells it to, I said no to the termination, at least until they were sure the baby was dead or I was actually dying. Currently I was just in severe pain, and I knew the pain itself wouldn't kill me. I knew they would monitor me, and I knew our community and church would pray for me and this baby. We settled into the hospital to wait for my body to miscarry naturally or for the baby to miraculously move.

Ectopic rupture is the leading cause of death among pregnant women in their first trimester, and there are only three known cases of an ectopic pregnancy resulting in a healthy birth. I knew I was asking for a nearly impossible thing. But there was a sure belief in me that if God's nearness was my good, and if he was good and all he did was good and sufficient, than this was somehow good and sufficient too. Something about this out-of-place baby was not only teaching me of God's goodness; it was also in itself somehow intrinsically good. Even if we lost the baby, we could trust God to be good. Our hope was in him, not in the outcome we most immediately wanted.

We spent the week praying, weeping, believing, and in doubt. Our church family surrounded us with prayer and presence, Matt and Lauren Chandler and their kids laid hands on us and prayed, our elders texted and called us, and our home group cared for all our needs. There were moments of clarity in my morphined mind when I just believed God was going to move the baby into my uterus. And there were other moments where I just wanted it to be over. Our doctors sometimes had good news ("Things are looking good today. I knew a patient once where I saw the sac on her tube one day, and the next week it was in her uterus!") and sometimes bad ("I'm pretty concerned about the swelling of your tube and the amount of pain you're in.") I remembered Matt, right after his cancer diagnosis, sharing his prayer with us: "God, I believe you can heal and I'm going to ask that you would heal, and I'm going to trust you even if you don't heal." We postured our hearts in submission to God, begging for the impossible but trusting him with the probable.

A week later, my already naturally low blood pressure was dropping, the pain wasn't abating, and the risk was too high. They surgically removed my ruptured fallopian tube and the dead baby.

GOOD AND ENOUGH

Grief is a strange thing, yet I am no stranger to it. But while grief means it feels as though something has been stolen, in some ways my grief this time brought something of a gift with it.

This is the nature of life in Christ—this is the great gospel paradox. Death in order to live (Revelation 1 v 18; John 12 v 24-25). Strength through weakness (2 Corinthians 12 v 10). Last in order to be first (Matthew 20 v 16). I knew the sufficiency of Christ, but I did not know the agonizing work of asking with full belief. All my past asking had been coupled with doubt, caveated by "if it's your will..." This asking had been bold, forthright, out-loud, and I still hadn't gotten the answer I wanted.

Dayenu, daughter, the Lord reminded me. *Is the answer sufficient? Is this answer sufficient? Even if it's not the one you wanted? Am I enough?* And somehow, he was and it was. Maybe for the first time.

Grief was profound, and I mourned hard and long, months longer than for any of our miscarriages. But somewhere in there, like a seed thrown on a pile of dirt, there was a goodness, and a trust in God, and, from our perspective, a willingness to put our desires to rest.

For whatever reason, my body is too high-risk for a baby. We could go through thousands of dollars and dozens of tests and multiple rounds of attempts to curve away from what God has not given us, and we could still not have children. Or we could trust that God builds families in different ways, through different means; and sometimes those means are fostering or adoption. Or sometimes simply childlessness.

Infertility—or, in our case, being fertile but unable to carry—doesn't mean God is withholding his blessing. We are trusting that our inability to have children is his blessing—and therefore, all he does within this space is also his blessing. It's not emptiness to him. It's not wasted space or out of place or not enough. He's working and weaving and speaking his blessing to us in the midst of all the spaces where we feel void.

Sometimes God says to a man and a woman, *This is sufficient. Together, the two of you, because I am near you and Christ has come, this is enough. This is good and enough.* Not second-best, not runner-up, not settled-for, not "We'll take what we can get." This is sufficient because God is in it, and he is near, and every promise in him is yes and amen, good and enough. Good enough.

November 12, 2010

It's hard to believe that we're coming up on one year.

We've been thinking quite a bit about that. A ton of things have happened this year, and so we've started to kind of think through some of those things and thank God for his mercies throughout the year, both in the bad news at the beginning of the year and then on into the good news in this year's closing out.

We had an MRI today and they used perfusion, which shows activity in regards to whether or not the cells are getting blood and if cancer cells are trying to get blood in order to multiply quickly. The scan came back 100% clean. So really for the first time throughout this whole thing, the doctors were visibly excited by the scan, as if they think we've beat this thing—although they were clear that they would never tell anybody that they wouldn't have a recurrence, because that's always a possibility. Because of the aggressive tactics of the doctors and then in the end what we know and understand to be our God's will, it looks like we're clean.

I have to continue on the regimen of chemo, and so I have nine rounds left, so I've got to kind of endure those, and I'd sure appreciate your prayers on those— they are not pleasant weeks.

So we celebrated tonight in this family and have just been enjoying the Lord and what appears to be, right now, the Lord saying that if my life is cut short, it won't be because of this brain cancer. So thank you for your prayers—I just feel indebted to the Lord, and also to you guys for just so faithfully pestering the King of heaven on my behalf.

11. HE WEPT WITH ME

Joy in the Sorrow of a Husband's
Brain Tumor

Lauren Chandler

My mother would be the first to tell you that she is a worst-case-scenario type of person. To be fair, that's what happens when your father owns and operates a funeral home. From the time she could spell her name, death was an everyday reality.

This might explain why I know more than I want to about the various ways someone might die (and why, to this day, my mom wants me to call or text her when I reach my destination on a road trip). You would think this would paralyze me with fear, but for the most part, I have lived my life believing that it would go along as comfortably as possible.

Looking back, my rosy worldview was epitomized by a comment I made as I sat across from my pastor's wife as a newly married nineteen-year-old. We'd found a cozy spot in an old farmhouse turned tea-room and nestled in for a long lunch. Our conversation covered everything from my speech pathology classes and her kids' latest hi-jinks, to dreams and plans for the future. Toward the end, we spoke about a family in the church who were enduring suffering. I furrowed my brow and sighed as she related the details. We sat in silence for a moment.

I didn't have much of a theology of suffering then. There simply didn't seem enough time to think about it, nor any pressing need to do so. My life seemed to lay before me pregnant with promise, all of it going according to plan. When I finally opened my mouth, I uttered words that cause me to cringe now:

"I think my life will go along pretty smoothly. It has so far!"

I've often wondered what my pastor's wife was thinking. She was too kind to burst my bubble. She may have tried to gently deflate it, but I didn't have ears to hear. Most of us don't like to think about suffering until it comes knocking.

THANKSGIVING DAY 2009
Fast forward a decade, and it's Thanksgiving Day 2009. By now, I had had a fair share of suffering. I had lost grandparents, experienced two miscarriages, and watched my eighteen-month-old son shake and convulse with a febrile seizure. I held him in my arms, strapped to a gurney, as we were carried away in an ambulance. Ten years had done a humbling work on that starry-eyed newlywed—but nothing would shape me like the season that began that Thursday in November.

It was like any other crisp fall morning. I had crept out of bed to begin making my share of the Thanksgiving menu while the rest of the family slept. Audrey bounced out of bed first with every ounce of six-year-old enthusiasm. Four-year-old Reid and thirty-five-year-old Matt followed closely behind but with only a fraction of Audrey's energy. Norah, barely six months old, eventually summoned us with a "Hey, I'm awake!" cry from her crib.

Matt cuddled and fed Norah a bottle in his usual spot in the living room—a well-worn, hand-me-down armchair with classic 1960's harvest gold and cream stripes. Meanwhile, the older kids spotted and subsequently celebrated their favorite cartoon characters in float form in the Thanksgiving parade on television. I was in the kitchen finishing up breakfast.

A clatter from the living room interrupted the steady hum of the oven. I knew something was wrong when I heard Audrey's voice calling for Matt, who had just been sitting next to her. He was still in the room—but he was on the floor, having a grand mal seizure. Our kids were somewhat oblivious to what was happening to Matt. Still, I shielded his shaking body from their eyes. I frantically ordered Audrey to find my phone and bring it to me immediately. We lived so close to the fire station that I could hear the ambulance sirens turn on when I called 911. My parents lived just as close and pulled in not long after I called them once the EMTs had arrived. They took the kids home with them while I got into the front of the ambulance and my husband was loaded in the back.

Matt had stopped seizuring while I was on the phone with dispatch, and he began to wake up as they secured him in the ambulance. I remember sitting in the front seat of the truck and thinking, "I never imagined myself sitting here, in this place, for this reason." He was thirty-five. I was twenty-nine. But here we were. I wondered if life would ever be the same. Would my husband ever recover? Would the rest of our lives be spent with me caring for him? Yet even in that moment, with those questions racing around, the one thing I knew for sure was that the Lord would give me the grace required.

While most families were sitting around tables enjoying turkey, dressing, and all the trimmings, ours was split between an exam room in the ER and a table in my parents' home with two empty chairs. I held Matt's hand as he became lucid. He asked me several times how he had gone from his cozy armchair to a hospital bed. The staff shuffled him in and out of the room for different tests and scans until the doctor pulled up a chair to the side of Matt's bed and sat down. His previously tough and pragmatic tone turned tender. One of the scans revealed a large mass in Matt's right frontal lobe. He recommended that we find a neurosurgeon quickly. We knew there was something seriously wrong, but we were just so ready to be home. All we wanted at that moment was to have the family together—to have some semblance of normalcy. We didn't realize then how long that would take to regain.

DO THE NEXT THING

The weekend limped on. We tried not to think too much about the upcoming appointment with the neurosurgeon. We were terrible at the not thinking. Matt had it in his mind that there would be a simple explanation—that the tumor was something to be watched but not worried about. I wasn't so sure. I had a feeling it was serious and that we seriously needed to attend to it.

Dr. Barnett's office was already decked in Christmas cheer. We stepped past tinsel and evergreen garlands into his consultation room. He invited us to sit down within view of his computer screen, and dimmed the lights as our eyes focused on the screen.

The mass was so large that even I could spot it.

It was evident that Dr. Barnett didn't think this was a "wait-and-see" type of tumor. Before the gravity of the situation could hit us, he explained how he had made room in his surgery schedule so Matt could have an operation and start his rehabilitation before Christmas.

Surgery? Rehab? Only a few days earlier we had been out-lining our upcoming trip to Disney World over the break. Now we were planning at least a week-long hospital stay? The mental and emotional whiplash was overwhelming.

Stunned and a bit dazed, we moved through the rest of the day's pre-op appointments. The most tender moment came when Matt called his dear friend and fellow lead pastor, Josh. I could only hear Matt's side of the conversation, but I could imagine Josh's voice in gentle tones and words.

"I can get through this; I know that," Matt confessed, "It's just... what about my kids? Will they hate God for this? Will they blame him? That I could not get through."

Yes, I thought: *that we could not bear.*

Although my theology of suffering was still forming, my faith in the Lord's goodness was secure. I had known his kindness and love in sending Jesus to live the life I failed to live and die the death I knew I deserved. I had known the ministry of the Holy Spirit—an inexplicable presence in my time of need. My kids, however, were just beginning to understand God's character. They were learning that he is good, wise, generous, kind, sovereign, and loving. They were hearing that, at church and at home. But... how could their burgeoning faith withstand the suffering and possible death of their father? I could not dwell there. I had to wrap up the questions and worries and lay them right at the Lord's feet. *Lord, he is yours. I'm yours. They're yours. I trust you.* I knew we would come back and address them, but for now there was work to do.

Elisabeth Elliot was a woman well acquainted with suffer-ing. In the 1950s, she and her husband, Jim, left everything familiar to reach a remote tribe in Ecuador with the gospel. Less than a year from when he and four other male mis-sionaries made initial contact with the group of natives, they were killed by the very people they'd come to help. Elisabeth

"I could trust Jesus
with the 'what ifs'
and 'tomorrows,' and,
by his grace, do what
needed to be done."

JOYINTHESORROW

was left behind, a widow after only three years of marriage and the single mother of a 10-month-old girl. When asked about seasons of suffering, depression, or anxiety, she often referred to a repeated phrase in an old, anonymous poem: "Do the next thing."

> *Many a questioning, many a fear,*
> *Many a doubt, hath its quieting here.*
> *Moment by moment, let down from Heaven,*
> *Time, opportunity, guidance are given.*
> *Fear not tomorrows, child of the King,*
> *Trust them with Jesus, do the next thing.*

On the drive home from Dr. Barnett's office, I realized I could not sit under the weight of the "what ifs." I wasn't in denial, but I was grateful for a to-do list. There were three children at home dependent upon me to make sure they were taken care of. I could trust Jesus with the "what ifs" and "tomorrows," and, by his grace, do what needed to be done.

So that's what we did. We trusted, and we did the next thing. Matt rested, healed (from the head wound he'd suffered during his seizure), and got his work in order at the church. I gathered schedules and schoolwork and made sure the kids were ready for our departure. I wasn't sure how long we would be at the hospital, but I knew I wanted to be with Matt—whatever and however long that meant.

WE NEEDED OUR PEOPLE

Our church gathered around and upheld us. We couldn't have endured this season without them. We were showered with prayers, meals, gift cards, babysitting, and, most importantly, presence. When we arrived at the hospital in the early hours before Matt's surgery, our closest friends and family were there waiting for us. And when Matt was rolled to the operation room, they sat with me for the duration of his eight-hour resection. They held their breath with me every time the nurse called to give an update. And they cheered with me when we heard he was able to recognize his surgeon upon waking. The words of the wise king Solomon rang true:

> Two are better than one, because they have a good reward for their toil. For if they fall, one will lift up his fellow. But woe to him who is alone when he falls and has not another to lift him up! Again, if two lie together, they keep warm, but how can one keep warm alone? And though a man might prevail against one who is alone, two will withstand him—a threefold cord is not quickly broken.
> (Ecclesiastes 4 v 9-12)

We often read these words at weddings, but they're not for married couples primarily. They're for all of us. We were created for community—with God and with one another. We need each other. Matt and I needed our people. We needed friends to lift us up and keep us warm on one of our darkest nights. We needed them to stand with us against the lies of the enemy—that the Lord is not good, that he would forsake us in the midst of this trial. We needed them to pray for healing and to be the hands and feet of Jesus to us. We certainly needed them over the next eighteen months.

HE KNEW WHO I WAS

Word finally came that Matt was resting in the neuro-intensive care unit. I couldn't wait to lay eyes on him. At the same time, I was afraid of what I might see. Would he look like himself? Would I see the characteristic sparkle in his eye? Would he recognize me? *Would he remember who I was?*

Matt gave me the biggest smile he could manage, fresh from anaesthesia.

"Hey, Boo!"

I melted. He knew who I was!

His head was wrapped several times with a large white bandage. He looked a bit like Sports Goofy after a fall (don't tell him I told you that). But honestly, he could have been swaddled from head to toe and I wouldn't have cared, as long as he was all there.

Our people came in a few at a time. Matt did what he does—cracked jokes and tried to make everyone else comfortable. No matter how hard he tried, though, everyone knew about the long road ahead. They saw their able-bodied pastor and fearless leader weak and frail. Although this is essentially Matt's story of suffering, it's also mine and our family's. And I cannot forget that it also belongs to the people whose lives God has allowed Matt to touch.

We didn't bring the kids to see him until he was much further along in his recovery. As much as we could, we wanted to keep their perception of Daddy close to what they'd known. The bandages, tubes, and wires were overwhelming, and it seemed like he wouldn't need them for too long.

The days and nights in neuro-ICU were a blur. Nurses and visitors came and went. Machines beeped. Vitals were monitored, medicine administered. Neither of us got sufficient sleep. My family convinced me to take advantage of the hotel room reserved for me in the hospital. Although my body lay in the comfort of one room, my heart and mind were with Matt in his. Nights were the hardest. The vulnerable stage between wakefulness and sleep was set for fear to step in. All the questions I pushed away during waking hours returned in full force. If it weren't for a dear friend who prayed out loud over me as I fell asleep, I'm not sure I would have caught a wink. The prayers of the saints were tangible. I look back on those days with wonder at how we endured. I am convinced it was God's kindness and grace through intercessory prayers lifted up from all over the world.

Matt was moved from neuro-ICU to a regular hospital room only a few days after surgery. We were grateful for the break from constant monitoring, but there was something comforting about a nurse's watchful eye that I missed.

Should this be beeping?

What does this light mean?

The staff weren't as anxious to check on him. I tried to convince myself that this must be an indication that he was doing OK. It didn't really work.

TWO TO THREE YEARS

We continued to have visitors daily. Friends and family made their way down from the suburbs to the heart of the city. Pastors from area churches took time away from their duties, families, and congregants to check on Matt—to pray with and over him. One pastor brought his pre-teen son. He, his son, and Matt chatted about the latest college football game. I could tell it was a welcome distraction.

The one visitor we were most anxious for was Dr. Barnett. He usually came in with a cheery disposition and a hot cup of coffee for Matt. What I wanted him to bring was good news, or at least word on the pathology of the tumor.

One day, I followed him out the door into the hallway.

"When will we know something?"

"I have a friend looking at the report right now. We are waiting on a few more samples before we can settle on the pathology."

I wanted to be hopeful, but it seemed to me that the longer they took, the grimmer the outcome might be. I was not holding my breath for good news, but I wasn't ruling it out either. I knew that anything was possible with God. I was reminded of a friend's prayer for Matt the night before his surgery, when she had echoed the Lord's question to Abraham in Genesis 18 v 14: "Is anything too hard for the LORD?" Was a little thing like a tumor too hard for the Lord? Was cancer too hard for him? Was healing too hard for him? Was sustaining Matt, me, and our family through the fiery trial of brain cancer too hard for him?

No, it wasn't. It still isn't. Nothing is too hard for the Lord.

I knew that in my head. I so desperately wanted to know it in the depths of my soul. The Lord was abundantly kind to use this crisis to integrate what I believed in my mind and what I was convinced of in my heart.

Dr. Barnett called the next day to set up a meeting. He wanted to discuss the pathology report in person.

Lord, I need you, I prayed.

My parents, Matt's parents, and my closest friends gathered in the foyer of the hospital cafeteria. There was a hallway full of meeting rooms on one side. Dr. Barnett invited Brian Miller (one of our lead pastors) and me into a room. Throat tight and heart racing, I had to remind myself to breathe. The conference room was already small, and it felt like the walls were inching in.

"I've got the report," Dr. Barnett said solemnly. "The tumor is oligodendroglioma. It's anaplastic. Malignant."

I don't know if it was the interminable wait for the results or purely the grace of God, but I wasn't surprised. I knew it wasn't good. Even from the very first meeting with the surgeon, I had known it was something serious. What knocked the breath out of me was his answer to my next question.

"What's the life expectancy?"

"Two to three years."

Was this really happening? Did his words mean what I thought they meant? I imagine I looked like the person in a film who's just been shot—the shock, the delay in response, and then the crumpling realization. No matter how many movies or TV shows you've seen where people receive devastating news, you can't really prepare yourself to hear the words in real life—in your real life, about the real life of someone you love. But I can say this without hesitation—Jesus was with me in that moment. I believe he wept with me in that moment, just like he did with his friends Mary and Martha when their brother Lazarus died (John 11 v 35). As Brian's arms wrapped around me and we both shook with tears, I believe Jesus was there with us, crying with us.

Once we pulled ourselves together, Dr. Barnett gave us further instructions. He wanted Matt to focus on recovery, so he asked that we delay telling him the results for a week. Of all the trying parts of our season of suffering, holding onto this secret was the hardest. Matt was and is my best friend. I'm great at keeping secrets that are good surprises. This was not that. It was a burden I bore alone. Although, praise God, not completely alone. The Lord invited me to trust him with it. When I had no one else to turn to, when my dearest confidante on earth was withheld, I had him. I had his word and the comfort of the knowledge of the Spirit's presence, even when I couldn't feel him.

There was more to Dr. Barnett's directions. While Matt worked hard in rehab, I was tasked with making appointments with the neuro-oncologist and neuro-radiation oncology specialist. I welcomed the "next things" to do. They gave me a sense of purpose and direction. I felt like I was helping fight the battle alongside Matt. I knew most of the battle would be Matt's to fight, but I wanted to do something.

Matt was able to come home a week before Christmas. He had handled the news of his diagnosis and prognosis well.

The man I believed him to be was proven in this trial. Although he was weak, in flesh and in spirit, he threw himself wholly on the grace of God. He never quit trusting that the Lord's steadfast love would sustain him and our family.

The Advent season took on greater depth and texture that year. Advent was not invented simply as the season where we race around, trying to be ready for Christmas. It is intended to be a time of looking toward Christ's future coming, before we celebrate his coming in the past—a time of waiting for the Messiah who will free us from bondage, the King who will establish his perfect kingdom on earth. The longing for Christ's second advent, when he comes "a second time, not to deal with sin but to save those who are eagerly waiting for him" (Hebrews 9 v 28), had become more acute. That year, I learned to ache for his return. The clouds of night and shadows of death lurked around the edges of our lives. Jesus was truly our only hope. I could hardly sing the words to "O Come, O Come Emmanuel" without tears.

> O come, Thou Dayspring, come and cheer
> Our spirits by Thine advent here,
> Disperse the gloomy clouds of night,
> And death's dark shadows put to flight.

WITH YOU, EVEN IN THE DARK

As January came, each day it got easier to find the rhythm in our "new normal." We made a schedule for people who wanted to take Matt to his appointments. Of course, I went most of the time. Matt's strength dwindled with each radiation treatment, but he always got to come home and rest. I know that's not always the case for cancer patients. A dear young woman named Stephanie helped me with the kids, who continued living life as usual. They knew their daddy wasn't feeling well but couldn't comprehend the extent. Reid had baseball games. Audrey had play dates. Norah had nap time. Matt was present when he could be. I leaned on Stephanie, my family, and dear friends. The Lord carried us all.

For eighteen months, Matt received treatment: six weeks of radiation, six weeks of low-dose chemo, and high-dose for the remainder. Each month he had an MRI scan and follow-up with Dr. Fink, the neuro-oncologist. I steeled myself for the results every time. Would they find something? Would the tumor return? Would there be a new concern?

If I could receive bad news once and live, I could do it again. *My God is able.*

For the entirety of the treatment, my fears were never realized. Matt had clear scan after clear scan. For ten years now, there has been no recurrence of disease. I wish we could say that he's in remission. But the reality of a primary brain tumor is that medical professionals don't get to say that. Statistically, there's always a chance of recurrence.

But God.

He doesn't work according to statistics. Nothing is too hard for him. He can keep rogue brain cells at bay. He can preserve Matt's life. We believe that. We trust that even if he chooses to do something otherwise, he will give us the grace to endure. What's more, he will be with us in the midst of it.

I want every story to end like ours. I want those who hear the frightening word "cancer" to know that God is able to heal and deliver. I want to see them fight victoriously through chemo and radiation, or not even need treatment at all! But more than I want healing and victory, I want them to know the presence and the goodness and the peace of God in the midst of their trial. He is the God who is with us whether or not we see the outcome we want in this life.

He is with us in the loss as much as the healing. He is with us as we face death, and through death, and beyond death. For those who have trusted in Jesus and have turned to him for salvation and hope, we can cling to his promise in the darkest night:

> *And behold, I am with you always, to the end of the age. (Matthew 28 v 20)*

12. THE SPIRIT'S SURGERY

Joy in the Sorrow of
a Brain Tumor

Matt Chandler

The day after that Thanksgiving, I woke up to see a couple of my closest friends and my bride. I had no memory of the seizure—only a foggy head and sharp pains in my mouth that made swallowing agony (turns out I had bitten through my tongue during the episode).

The doctor pulled a small stool up next to my bed and informed me that the CT scan that I had no memory of had revealed a shadow in my brain, and they had ordered an MRI. I didn't care. I wanted to go home. The thought that my children had watched me have a grand mal seizure on Thanksgiving morning was all that went through my mind and heart as they pinned down my head with a plastic halo and eased me into the MRI machine. My shoulders rounded up, and a brief moment of panic overtook me. I felt trapped and alone. If you have ever watched me preach, you'll know that asking me to keep still for 45 minutes will require a miracle. Yet on that afternoon, I lay there utterly motionless.

The next month was a whirlwind of fear, physical pain and spiritual longing. We found a surgeon, I survived an eight-hour craniotomy, and we learned two new words: "anaplastic oligodendroglioma." We also learned all about WHO grades of tumor. We named the tumor in my right frontal lobe Keyser Söze, after the fictional character and main antagonist in the film *The Usual Suspects*. "Keyser" was a WHO grade III, which meant he was malignant, and I was given the prognosis of two to three years. It's hard to communicate the lows and then the depths of that month and the months that followed. It felt like the floor fell out of the bottom, and we were free-falling.

They had cut out most of my right frontal lobe, and part of rehab after brain surgery is to be given lots of things that stress out the rest of your brain, so that it learns to come and help the damaged part. They made me draw with my "wrong" hand. I had to use tweezers to pick up pushpins and drop them in a Styrofoam cup, for hours. And I had to answer questions that made links between objects.

So they would say, "Which one of these items doesn't belong: a chainsaw, a knife and a fork?" Now, most people will say, "The chainsaw. You eat dinner with a knife and a fork, and you don't eat dinner with the chainsaw." I thought, "Well, the knife and the chainsaw both cut. So it's the fork. The fork doesn't belong." And I would argue my point. Lauren was trying to help: "Matt, think about it—we're at dinner: which of these won't you find on the table?" And I was just doubling down, being stubborn, insisting that "fork" was the answer (At that point, she was like, *Matt's fine... Yeah, Matt's back.*)

But I did well overall on the tests, and after a week the hospital thought I was good to go, but I think Lauren got in their ear and was just like, "Look, I've got three babies at home. And he doesn't know the difference between a fork and a chainsaw…" She was worried that I would try to carry Norah upstairs, so she wanted me to get stronger before I came home, which was smart because you don't know what you don't know after somebody's messed with your brain. The strength and dignity and wisdom that Lauren exhibited in those early weeks still brings tears to my eyes all these years later.

So it was that I was released from the hospital after some neurological rehab and went home just a few days before Christmas, and that's when the Spirit started to do some surgery of his own.

WHY NOT THIS MAN?

It was the holidays, and I gently sat down on the large leather couch in front of our mantel. Lauren, over time, had turned our living room into something you might find in a cottage in rural France (or at least, what I imagine cottages look like there). Our hearth was made of large Oklahoma flagstones, and the mantel was made of giant cedar beams that my father-in-law and I personally "distressed." We spent hours making those new beams look like old beams before we installed them. It was the first time I noticed that, in the middle of what was the most stressful and fearful few weeks of our lives, my in-laws, some friends and Lauren had decorated our home for Christmas and had done an extraordinary job.

The mantel was covered with those pictures of our friends and acquaintances that seem to have become commonplace on the front of Christmas cards. Among dozens and dozens of photos, my eyes met those of one man, and the Spirit made his first really deep incision. I nearly screamed.

It wasn't blood that poured out of the wound—it was anger, entitlement and self-righteousness. The eyes that caught mine were those of a man with a stunningly beautiful family. They were wealthy, attended church regularly, and looked the part of the Dallas suburban scene. But behind that touched-up photo there was a real darkness: a narcissistic husband and father who couldn't seem to stay faithful, who emotionally manipulated and tormented his family, and walked in a smug arrogance that was visible. When our eyes met, the thought exploded out of my heart:

"Really, God?! Me? You're going to let me die in my 30s. Why not this man?!"

The rest of my thoughts will need to be filtered for this chapter, but it was ugly. This wasn't good, biblical lament. This was evil and darkness seeping out from the crevices of my soul.

At first I felt no rebuke or shame, just pride. Like a fool who knew deep down his argument was weak and baseless, I stood my ground, spiritual arms crossed, feeling justified. But when I was done thrashing about and realized the foolishness of what I was saying to the Author and Creator of the universe, the One who sits outside of time, who has always been and will always be, I received what I shouldn't have: mercy.

Just as the MRI had revealed the tumor in my brain, this moment on the couch revealed my pride and my self-righteousness. I realized that I believed God owed me: that I had put God in my debt with all my preaching, leading, and serving; that I had earned comfort, influence, and health. There was a visible pride in my living room that day, and it was mine. The Spirit had just done his own MRI, and I was sick. I sat there dumbstruck as God the Father, through his Son and by his Spirit, brought to my mind all that I had studied, read and taught over the previous years, and I started to sob uncontrollably. The mercy and grace I experienced in that moment has marked me forever.

In John 15, Jesus teaches that the Father will prune fruitful branches and cut off fruitless branches. I found myself in the middle of being pruned. I think I understand better now why the fruitful branches get pruned. I was fruitful but sick, walking in the sins of ignorance and immature attitudes without being able to see them. There was an insidious spiritual sickness in my soul, and my Father loved me too much to let it grow. Like the cancer in my brain, this disease of the heart needed to be cut out.

The Bible is filled with warnings against pride and the rebellion that flows from it. In Psalm 138 v 6, King David writes, "For though the LORD is high, he regards the lowly, but the haughty he knows from afar." God will be near to the lowly. He "regards" them, which means to have attention, concern, to have their best interests in view. This is how God sees the humble.

The haughty or proud, though, "he knows from afar." There is a distance that harms them—a gap between Creator and creation, robbing his creatures of joy. In the same way that my doctor removed that golf-ball-sized anaplastic WHO grade III oligodendroglial tumor, God in his mercy desired to reveal my pride and start the process of removing it. The cut was deep and painful but necessary for me if I was to truly heal. Like the cancer, it had grown undetected.

That was the lesson of the couch. There would be more to learn.

THE LESSON OF THE BACK ROW

The first real outing I had was on Christmas Eve, to the services at The Village. As I sat in the row right at the back of the building, I could hardly hold it together. It's hard to keep it together at Christmas when you've just heard the words, "You have a couple of years to live." It was a difficult Christmas. I was wondering if it was going to be my last. My family was wondering if it was going to be my last.

But it was OK.

It was OK because the tumor, which was spoiling that Christmas and threatening to finish my life, didn't take away my hope. You feel the beauty of the first Christmas more clearly when you don't know how many more you'll see. You know how much it matters that God has got involved in this world and in our lives and has put an anchor down for our souls, regardless of our circumstances. As I sat in the back row, tears streaming down my face, I didn't know what would happen. But I did know this: it was going to be OK.

That Christmas it snowed a ton—the kind of real, legitimate, you-can-actually-build-something-out-of-this snow that we almost never get in Texas. On Christmas Day, the kids were outside playing. I couldn't do anything because of the surgery. You don't want to slip on the ice after that. All I could do was watch from inside, slightly dazed.

And here's what I can tell you. The peace of God was thick. Things were hard. But Jesus was enough. He was with me. He comforted me. He gave me joy. He gave me hope.

THE LESSON OF THE BED

One of the kindest things the Lord showed me in that season was that anxiety was not going to be a war that he would let me win—it was going to be a battle that he would let me fight. As Christians, we're commanded, "Do not be anxious about anything" (Philippians 4 v 6). And I learned that this, at least for me, required an ongoing struggle in which it would rarely be easy to obey, but that God was going to meet me in real special ways in that battle.

Sometimes, I felt like really it didn't matter what happened—"If it's glory, it's glory," I'd think. "If it's life, it's life—if it's death, it's death." Then in a matter of hours, with nothing happening to tip the scale, I'd go from that to being terrified of the ordeal. I remember one night in particular, laying in bed and being so frustrated with having to fight

"You feel the beauty of the first Christmas more clearly when you don't know how many more you'll see. I didn't know what would happen. But I did know this: it was going to be OK."

#JOYINTHESORROW

anxiety again. I thought I should know better. I thought, *I've taught on this stuff, so surely I shouldn't be wrestling with anxiety.* Lauren was already sleeping soundly next to me, and she was exhausted—I didn't want to wake her up and talk through it. So I prayed—and the Lord gave me a sense that I was being taught, as Moses put it, to number my days (Psalm 90 v 12); that the Lord was allowing me to stand on that precipice, and was working in me in that anxiety for things that I was going to need moving forward. He would help me battle—and work in me as I battled—for the good works he had laid out before me.

And it was actually in those wrestles with anxiety that I first got the sense that the Lord was going to heal me—that he was accomplishing something, and it was going to be something he used in this life. That in itself sent my mind all over the place: "Wait, am I in denial right now? Am I alright now? Is this the way other cancer guys have gone? Have they played this game? Hang on—if I'm sensing the Lord is going to heal me, am I a prosperity-gospel guy? If I am, I'm in the wrong church, and I'm its pastor!"

But in all of those battles with anxiety, with my own thoughts, as I lay there in bed God was coming close to me. He was there with me, teaching me to number my days, and showing me what really counted in each of those days, however many or however few they might be.

USE YOUR DAYS

I was more aware of the things I had studied and taught after that Christmas Eve on the back row, after that day on the couch during the holidays, and after those long nights in bed when the anxiety would rear up again. And even though I would still battle with pride, and with anxiety and fear—and still do sometimes today—the Lord was near to me. He was enough. I began to powerfully and personally experience the things I had heard and watched others experience around their suffering.

I wish I could say that the medical community has cleared me, and that there is nothing for me to be worried about, but even with ten years of clean scans and total health, no one has told me to relax. Twice a year, I go in for MRIs, and twice a day I take anti-seizure meds. My doctors continue to wait for the cancer to return. While I believe that I've been healed, they remain somewhat skeptical of my future.

Some pretty significant things happen when you've looked over that precipice—not least in discovering what really is important and whether or not the way you're spending your life is how you want to spend your life. For me, once I was basically better, there was a real question of "OK, how do I want to spend my days now?" They're precious and they're going fast, and so what do I want to do with them? The answer for me has been to really kind of shrink back and travel way less, to be present at TVC way more, and be in my family as much as possible. I have three circles—family, then TVC, and then Acts 29, the church-planting network I serve—and that's how I'm spending my life. All the other stuff is secondary. I get a lot of good opportunities, and that stuff can be intoxicating. But I know where my heart is; I know what I'm trying to build, and I can't build what I think the Lord has for me to build here in Dallas if I'm always out there. I've learned to number my days, and a part of numbering them well is to use them well.

RUN TO GOD

God used my bout with cancer to lower me, to change me, and to exalt himself. Now I'm sure there is much in me that the Lord wants to continue removing and healing, but the lessons of the back row, the bed, and (most of all, I think) the couch remain. What that spiritual MRI showed me continues to haunt me in the best possible ways. I continue to pray for myself what Moses prays: "Teach us to number our days that we may get a heart of wisdom" (Psalm 90 v 12). Every time I get a headache, or my hand tingles a bit, or I randomly feel dizzy, or I get an allergy attack, I remember. I am finite; he is infinite. He has my days, and he is good. I remember the back row, the couch, and the bed. I remember that the Spirit is with me, and I lean into the One who has numbered my days.

The pastor and theologian Samuel Rutherford once said, "When I am in the cellar of affliction, I look for the Lord's choicest wines." Know that God is at work in the mess for your joy and his glory. I have learned in my own life, and I've seen in the lives of others, that we find our faith tested when we sin and when we suffer. Do we run to God in those times, or do we run from him? By his grace, at TVC we have learned to run towards him, and we have helped each other to run to his arms when we are at our weakest and most broken. It's where joy is to be found, even in—especially in—sorrow. At the crossroads of doubt, anger, and fear, choose to trust him and the good work he is accomplishing. Run to him.

And Lord, haste the day when the faith shall be sight,
The clouds be rolled back as a scroll;
The trump shall resound, and the Lord shall descend,
Even so, it is well with my soul.

CONTRIBUTORS

DAVID ROARK is Communications and Resources Director at The Village Church.

MATT CHANDLER is Pastor of The Village Church, and President of the Acts 29 church-planting network. He is the author of books including *The Explicit Gospel* and *Take Heart*.

JEANNE DAMOFF is Groups Minister at TVC's Dallas campus.

GUY DELCAMBRE is a member of TVC and a mentor in the Art House Dallas community. He is the author of *Earth and Sky*.

KYLE PORTER is Golf Writer for CBS Sports and an elder at Mosaic Richardson, Texas, a church plant of TVC.

ERIN BRINDLEY is a Ministry Assistant at TVC's Dallas campus.

CHARITY READY is Classes and Curriculum Minister at TVC's Fort Worth campus.

TEDASHII ANDERSON is a hip-hop artist and member of 116 Clique. He and his wife, **DANIELLE ANDERSON**, were members at TVC's Denton campus, and now live in Atlanta.

ANNE LINCOLN HOLIBAUGH is Elementary/Associate Minister at The Village Church Denton, a former campus of TVC.

JONATHAN WOODLIEF is Lead Mobilization Minister at TVC's Dallas campus.

LORE FERGUSON WILBERT is a member of TVC's Flower Mound campus. She blogs at sayable.net.

LAUREN CHANDLER is a singer and songwriter, and the author of *Steadfast Love* and *Goodbye to Goodbyes*. She is married to Matt.

the good book

COMPANY

BIBLICAL | RELEVANT | ACCESSIBLE

At The Good Book Company, we are dedicated to helping Christians and local churches grow. We believe that God's growth process always starts with hearing clearly what he has said to us through his timeless word—the Bible.

Ever since we opened our doors in 1991, we have been striving to produce Bible-based resources that bring glory to God. We have grown to become an international provider of user-friendly resources to the Christian community, with believers of all backgrounds and denominations using our books, Bible studies, devotionals, evangelistic resources, and DVD-based courses.

We want to equip ordinary Christians to live for Christ day by day, and churches to grow in their knowledge of God, their love for one another, and the effectiveness of their outreach.

Call us for a discussion of your needs or visit one of our local websites for more information on the resources and services we provide.

Your friends at The Good Book Company

thegoodbook.com | thegoodbook.co.uk
thegoodbook.com.au | thegoodbook.co.nz
thegoodbook.co.in